A Cybersecurity Leader's Journey

In today's cybersecurity landscape, the role of a cybersecurity leader goes beyond technical expertise. Communicating cybersecurity risks and initiatives to executives and boards demands a unique blend of strategic insight and business language. *A Cybersecurity Leader's Journey: Speaking the Language of the Board* takes readers on a transformative path from technical talk to business-savvy communication.

Follow Nick, a newly appointed CISO, as he navigates the challenges of bridging the gap between complex cybersecurity concepts and the business-focused concerns of board members. Struggling to convey the impact of cybersecurity initiatives, Nick quickly realizes that his technical knowledge alone isn't enough to gain the board's trust. With guidance from a mentor, he learns how to address the board's priorities, answer the critical question of "What's in it for me?", and deliver insights that resonate.

This book offers more than just a narrative—it provides actionable takeaways for cybersecurity leaders and other professionals who want to master the art of strategic communication. Readers will discover how to close information asymmetry gaps, manage the affect heuristic, and develop a communication style that builds trust and fosters informed decision-making.

Whether you're a CISO, an aspiring CISO, or a technical expert aiming to improve your business communication, *A Cybersecurity Leader's Journey* equips you with the skills to make cybersecurity not just a necessity but a valued component of business success as well. Step into Nick's journey, gain insights from his challenges, and learn how to become the trusted advisor your board needs.

Security, Audit and Leadership Series

Series Editor: Dan Swanson, Dan Swanson and Associates, Ltd., Winnipeg, Manitoba, Canada.

The Security, Audit and Leadership Series publishes leading-edge books on critical subjects facing security and audit executives as well as business leaders. Key topics addressed include Leadership, Cybersecurity, Security Leadership, Privacy, Strategic Risk Management, Auditing IT, Audit Management and Leadership

A Cybersecurity Leader's Journey

Speaking the Language of the Board

Dr. Edward Marchewka

CRC Press
Taylor & Francis Group
Boca Raton London New York

CRC Press is an imprint of the
Taylor & Francis Group, an **informa** business

Designed cover image: Shutterstock image 2234694081

First edition published 2025
by CRC Press
2385 NW Executive Center Drive, Suite 320, Boca Raton FL 33431

and by CRC Press
4 Park Square, Milton Park, Abingdon, Oxon, OX14 4RN

CRC Press is an imprint of Taylor & Francis Group, LLC

© 2025 Edward Marchewka

ISBN: 978-1-032-98053-9 (hbk)
ISBN: 978-1-032-98175-8 (pbk)
ISBN: 978-1-003-59740-7 (ebk)

DOI: 10.1201/9781003597407

Typeset in Adobe Casion
by Deanta Global Publishing Services, Chennai, India

For Natalie, Connor, and Kyle

Contents

Acknowledgments

Thanks to the Chicago CISO community for continued support and always being willing to listen and provide guidance.

Author Biography

Edward Marchewka, DBA, MBA, MS, CISSP, CDPSE, PMP, CMQ/OE, LSSMBB is an industry-recognized executive, having been the 2022 CIO of the Year Finalist and 2015 CISO of the Year Nominee, with more than two decades of experience in IT and information security. His background includes experiences from running his own computer support business to field service to Fortune 250 experience with Thermo Fisher Scientific. He ran information security for Chicago Public Schools, the third-largest school district in the country. His career started in the US Navy as an Electrician's Mate—Nuclear.

Dr. Marchewka is active in the IT and information security community, having served the Chicago Infragard Members Alliance for over nine years. He has presented at dozens of events, including Camp IT Conferences, (ISC)² Security Congress, ISACA, Secureworld, and Gartner's Security and Risk Management Summit. He is an advisor for Prairie State Community College's IT Program.

Dr. Marchewka holds a Doctorate in Business Administration from California Southern University and MBA and MS in Mathematics from Northern Illinois University. He earned a BA in Liberal Studies and a BS in Nuclear Engineering Technologies from Thomas Edison State College, NJ. He holds certificates in Nonprofit

Management and Leadership from the Kellogg School of Management at Northwestern University and a certificate in Contract Management from the University of California–Irvine. Dr Marchewka maintains several active IT, security, and professional certifications from (ISC)², ASQ, ITIL, PMI, ISACA, SSGI, Microsoft, and CompTIA.

THE FIRST BOARD MEETING

Nick adjusted his tie nervously as he stood outside the boardroom of MedTech Parts, a company known for supplying high-quality components for medical equipment. It was his first board meeting as the new CISO, and he felt a mix of excitement and anxiety. The transition from leading IT infrastructure to being a CISO had been swift and intense. He had always excelled in technical roles, but communicating complex cybersecurity issues to a group of senior executives was a new challenge.

MedTech Parts was not just any company. Its reputation for excellence in the medical device industry meant that its products were integral to the functioning of critical healthcare equipment worldwide. The stakes were high, and the board members were acutely aware of this. They knew that any disruption in their supply chain or any compromise in the integrity of their products could have far-reaching consequences, not only for their business but also for the lives of countless patients. This knowledge added to Nick's pressure. He knew he had to be at the top of his game.

Although Nick had attended numerous board meetings in the past, he had always been there to support the executive team, providing technical expertise and backing up information when needed. This time, however, he was the one at the front, responsible for leading the discussion and ensuring that the board understood the critical importance of cybersecurity to the company's operations and reputation. The weight of this responsibility bore heavily on him. He knew that the board would scrutinize every word, every slide, and every piece of data he presented. They would not just be evaluating the cybersecurity measures; they would be evaluating him as well.

Nick had spent countless hours preparing his slide deck, filled with detailed technical metrics that he believed would showcase his expertise and the importance of cybersecurity. His journey to this moment

DOI: 10.1201/9781003597407-1

had been arduous but rewarding. He had spent the last few years developing robust metrics to measure the effectiveness of the cybersecurity initiatives he had implemented. Every vulnerability scanned, every patch applied, and every system secured was meticulously documented. These were his achievements, the tangible results of his hard work, and he was proud of them. Yet, as he stood outside the boardroom, he couldn't shake the feeling that something was missing.

For the last couple of months, his evenings and weekends had been consumed by an intense CISSP bootcamp, which he hoped would give him the edge he needed to be a successful CISO. He had attended numerous cybersecurity conferences to stay updated with the latest threats and defenses. At these conferences, speakers often emphasized the need to communicate in business terms but rarely provided concrete examples. There was a lot of discussion about the importance of metrics; however, the advice was often vague and not prescriptive enough to resonate with executives. Nick had listened to debates about the merits of qualitative versus quantitative approaches, but there was no clear consensus on which was better and why. Both methods had shortcomings, leaving Nick uncertain about how to frame his data effectively.

Nick's dedication to his role was evident in his meticulous approach. He had even invested time in developing a comprehensive cybersecurity dashboard visually representing the company's security posture. The dashboard included real-time metrics, trend analyses, and risk assessments. Nick believed that presenting this data to the board would demonstrate his proficiency and underscore the critical importance of cybersecurity in protecting the company's assets. However, as the meeting approached, he began to wonder if these metrics and graphs would be enough to convey the gravity of the situation to a board more concerned with the bottom line and operational efficiency.

As he entered the room, he was met with the familiar but stern faces of the board members, including the CEO, CFO, and other senior leaders. The room was formal and intimidating, with a large conference table, plush chairs, and a large screen displaying the presentations. The atmosphere was tense, and Nick could sense the high expectations. He realized that the boardroom was a battlefield, not just a place for discussion. Every word, every decision made here could significantly impact the company's future. The board members, seasoned professionals with years of experience, were not easily impressed. They had seen it all, from financial crises to market triumphs. For them, cybersecurity was just one more item on a long list of concerns. Nick knew he had to make it stand out.

Among the board members was Mike, a seasoned executive with a background in finance at Fortune 100 companies. Mike had a reputation for being highly analytical and detail oriented, with a keen eye for numbers and a deep understanding of financial impacts. He had joined MedTech Parts' board to help streamline operations and improve the company's financial health. Given his influential role in the company, Nick knew that impressing Mike would be crucial. Mike was the type of person who saw the world through spreadsheets and balance sheets. He needed to understand how every dollar spent on cybersecurity would save the company money in the long run. Nick had to find a way to translate his technical achievements into financial terms that Mike could appreciate.

"Good morning, everyone," Nick began, trying to keep his voice steady. "Today, I will be presenting our current cybersecurity status and the steps we are taking to mitigate risks."

He could feel the weight of their gazes on him, evaluating, judging. He clicked through his slides, each filled with charts and graphs showing the technical progress his team had made. He detailed the number of systems scanned, the vulnerabilities detected, and the patches applied. He explained the various cybersecurity tools and protocols his team had implemented. However, as he spoke, he noticed the board members exchanging puzzled glances and checking their phones. The sinking feeling in his stomach grew. He realized that he was losing them.

Mike leaned forward. "What does this mean for our bottom line?" he asked, his tone direct and to the point.

There was no room for fluff or vague explanations. Mike wanted numbers, projections, and a clear understanding of how cybersecurity would affect the company's financial health.

Nick paused, struggling to translate the technical details into business terms. "Well, reducing vulnerabilities helps prevent breaches, which can be costly," he replied, but his answer seemed to fall flat.

He knew it wasn't enough. The board didn't just want to know that cybersecurity was important; they wanted to know why it mattered to them, specifically in terms of dollars and cents.

Another board member, Kevin, frowned. Kevin was a logistics expert with broad global experience in moving products efficiently and cost-effectively. His deep understanding of supply chains and logistics operations made him an invaluable member of the board, especially for a company like MedTech Parts.

"How does this impact our ability to ship more products?" Kevin asked.

Nick felt a pang of frustration. He had prepared for technical questions but not for these business-centric concerns.

"A breach could disrupt operations and damage our reputation," he explained, but he could see that his answer wasn't satisfying the board.

They wanted specifics, not generalities. How would a cyber attack affect their supply chain? Would it delay shipments? Would it cost them customers? Nick realized he had focused too much on the technical side and not enough on the business impact.

Dr. Haversham, a physician and board member, leaned forward, their brow furrowed. Known for their intense focus on patient care and safety, they often asked questions that seemed tangential to the business at hand but were rooted in their medical background.

"Nick," they began, "how do your cybersecurity measures ensure that our components, when used in medical equipment, do not compromise patient safety? For instance, what if a cyber attack somehow impacted the functionality of these components?"

Nick hesitated, caught off guard by the question. He hadn't prepared for this angle.

"Well, Dr. Haversham, our main focus is on protecting our internal systems and data from breaches. By ensuring our manufacturing processes are secure, we...uh, we maintain the integrity of our processes."

But even as he said it, he knew it wasn't enough. The board needed more than assurances; they needed to understand how cybersecurity was directly linked to patient safety and the company's reputation in the healthcare industry.

Dr. Haversham didn't seem fully convinced.

"But what about the broader implications? Could a cyber breach affect the reputation of our components and indirectly affect patient safety through diminished trust in our products?"

Their voice was calm, but the underlying concern was clear. MedTech Parts' reputation in the medical industry was built on trust. If that trust was compromised, the consequences could be dire.

Nick struggled to find the right words.

"That's a good point. I suppose, in theory, if our systems were compromised, it could lead to concerns about the quality of our parts. But we have rigorous quality control measures in place to catch any issues."

He knew it wasn't enough. He needed to connect the dots between cybersecurity and patient safety in a way that resonated with the board.

Dr. Haversham nodded slowly but didn't seem entirely satisfied.

"I understand the focus on quality control, but it would be reassuring to know how these cybersecurity measures translate directly to ensuring patient safety and maintaining trust in our products."

Nick made a mental note to delve deeper into this area before the next meeting. He could feel the pressure of not fully addressing Dr. Haversham's concerns and knew he needed to prepare better for such questions in the future. The board was not just looking for technical solutions but for reassurance that every aspect of the company's operations, from manufacturing to logistics to customer trust, was being safeguarded.

The CEO, looking slightly impatient, chimed in.

"We need to understand the impact on our business operations. Can you provide a clearer picture?"

His tone was firm, and Nick could tell that time was running out. The CEO needed answers that would allow him to make informed decisions, not just a list of technical achievements.

Nick felt a wave of frustration and anxiety. Despite his best efforts, he couldn't seem to make the board understand the significance of his data. The meeting continued, but it was clear that the board members were confused and not fully engaged. Nick's slides, filled with technical jargon and complex metrics, weren't resonating with them. He realized he had focused too much on the details and not enough on the bigger picture. The board needed to see how cybersecurity fit into the company's overall strategy, how it supported the business goals, and how it protected its bottom line.

Nick felt a sinking feeling in his stomach as the meeting wrapped up. He knew that he had failed to communicate effectively. The board members filed out of the room, discussing other business matters, while Nick silently gathered his things. He couldn't shake the feeling that he had let them down. His technical expertise was not enough; he needed to find a way to translate that expertise into a language the board could understand.

Before Nick could leave, the COO, Sharon, pulled him aside. Sharon was known for her straightforward and practical approach.

"Nick," she began, "you need to button up your communication skills and connect better with the board. They need to understand how cybersecurity impacts our business directly. You have the technical expertise, but you need to translate that into something they can relate to. If you can't do that, we're going to have a hard time getting their support."

Nick nodded, feeling a mix of disappointment and determination.

"I understand, Sharon. I'll work on it." He knew she was right. He needed to find a way to bridge the gap between his technical knowledge and the board's business priorities.

She gave him an encouraging smile.

"I know you will. You're good at what you do. Just remember, they need to see how what you're doing affects the bottom line and operations. You'll get there."

Her words were reassuring, but Nick knew that the real work was just beginning.

Nick left the room, determined to find a better way to communicate cybersecurity risks. He realized that his role as a CISO was not just about protecting the company's systems; it was about translating that protection into tangible business benefits that the board could understand and support.

That evening, Nick reflected on the meeting as he sat in his apartment, a modest but comfortable space that he rarely had time to enjoy. His thoughts were consumed by the board's lack of understanding and engagement. He realized that his approach needed to change if he was going to succeed in his new role. The challenge was not just about cybersecurity; it was about communication, about telling a story that resonated with the board and connected the dots between technology and business.

Nick decided to reach out to his network for advice. He contacted former colleagues, mentors, and industry peers, hoping to find someone who had faced similar challenges. After a few conversations, he was directed to Kathy, an experienced CISO known for her ability to bridge the gap between technical and business leadership. Kathy was not just a cybersecurity expert; she was a communicator and a storyteller who knew how to translate technical details into business value.

Feeling a mix of hope and desperation, Nick sent Kathy an email outlining his situation and requesting a meeting. To his surprise, she responded quickly, agreeing to meet him the following week. Nick felt a sense of relief, knowing that he was not alone in this challenge.

As Nick prepared for the meeting with Kathy, he reviewed his presentation again, trying to see it from the board's perspective. He began to understand that while his technical achievements were significant, they needed to be framed to highlight their impact on the business. He needed to learn how to tell a compelling story that connected the dots between cybersecurity and business outcomes. The data alone was not enough; it needed to be contextualized and relevant to the board's concerns.

Nick felt a renewed sense of determination. He knew that this meeting with Kathy could be his needed turning point. It was time to learn from his mistakes and develop a communication strategy that resonated with the board and other key stakeholders. The journey ahead would be challenging, but Nick was ready to embrace it. This was not just about succeeding in his role as CISO; it was about becoming a leader who could bridge the gap between technology and business and communicating the importance of cybersecurity in a way that everyone could understand and appreciate.

Key Takeaways

1. **Understand Your Audience**: Tailor your communication to address the specific concerns and priorities of your audience.
2. **Simplify Technical Details**: Translate technical jargon into business-relevant terms that are easily understood by non-technical stakeholders.

3. **Focus on Business Impact**: Highlight how cybersecurity issues affect the business's bottom line and operational efficiency.
4. **Engage the Board**: Ensure that your presentation encourages questions and engagement from board members.
5. **Continuous Improvement**: Recognize the need for continuous improvement in communication strategies.

Discussion Prompts

1. What are the key challenges you face when communicating technical information to non-technical stakeholders?
2. How can you better align your cybersecurity presentations with the business priorities of your audience?

2
THE BREACH

The company's operations center was a hive of activity. Cybersecurity analysts worked frantically at their stations, their faces illuminated by the glow of multiple monitors. A significant data breach had just been detected, and the atmosphere was tense.

Nick stood in the center of the room, coordinating the response. His eyes scanned the monitors, taking in the flashing alerts and scrolling lines of code that filled the screens. Despite the chaos, he remained calm, his voice steady as he issued instructions. "We need to isolate the breach and secure our systems," he instructed, his voice calm but urgent. He had built a solid team, and their coordination and expertise were critical in moments like this. He had trained them well, preparing them for exactly this kind of scenario, and now their skills were being put to the test.

One of the analysts, Jane, looked up from her screen, her brow furrowed in concentration.

"We've isolated the breach, but it's going to take time to fully secure the system," she reported, her fingers still flying over the keyboard as she worked to implement the containment protocols.

Nick nodded, thinking quickly. Time was of the essence, and every second counted.

"Focus on containment for now. We need to minimize the damage," he responded, his mind racing through the next steps.

The breach was serious, and while they had managed to contain it, the real challenge would be in securing the compromised systems and ensuring that no further damage could be done.

As the team continued to work, Nick's boss, Mark, approached him with a concerned expression. Mark was a seasoned executive, with a deep understanding of the business and a keen sense of the implications of a breach like this.

DOI: 10.1201/9781003597407-2

"The board wants an update. How should we explain this?" Mark asked, his tone reflecting the gravity of the situation.

The board had been on high alert ever since Nick had taken on the CISO role, and now, with a breach occurring under his watch, the pressure was immense.

Nick sighed, his mind already turning over the challenge of communicating the situation to the board. He knew that the technical details, while important, would only confuse the board members, most of whom lacked a deep understanding of cybersecurity.

"I'll handle the communication," he assured Mark, his voice betraying none of the anxiety he felt.

This was his responsibility, and he knew he had to get it right. Nick headed toward his office, his thoughts racing. He knew the board would want answers—clear, concise, and, most importantly, relevant to the business. Quickly, he drafted an initial update, sticking to what he knew best: the technical details. But even as he typed, a nagging doubt crept in. He remembered the lessons from his first board meeting, where his focus on technical metrics had failed to resonate. He needed to do better this time.

He called for an immediate Zoom meeting with the board members, his heart pounding as he waited for them to join. As their faces appeared on the screen, Nick felt a familiar pang of nervousness, but he pushed it aside, focusing on the task at hand.

"Thank you for joining on such short notice," Nick began, his voice steady. "We've detected a significant data breach that has compromised sensitive customer information. Our team is working to contain the breach and secure our systems."

He watched the board members' faces closely, noting the tension and concern in their expressions. The board members looked anxiously at their screens.

"How bad is it?" the CEO asked.

"It's serious," Nick admitted, choosing his words carefully. "But we're doing everything we can to mitigate the impact."

He knew he had to strike a balance between honesty and reassurance. The last thing he wanted was to cause panic, but he also needed the board to understand the gravity of the situation.

Mike, the finance board member, spoke up, his face stern and his voice laced with concern.

"What are the immediate steps you're taking to secure our data?" he asked, his eyes narrowing as he leaned closer to the camera.

Mike was known for his meticulous attention to detail, especially when it came to financial risks. Nick knew he had to provide a clear and thorough explanation.

Nick outlined the containment measures, the additional monitoring being put in place, and the steps to identify and patch the vulnerability. He spoke with precision, detailing the technical actions his team had taken.

"We've also initiated an internal investigation to determine the scope of the breach and how it occurred," he added, knowing that this would be a critical part of the board's assessment of the situation.

Kevin, the logistics expert, leaned forward, his face serious.

"What about our operations? Will this impact our ability to ship products?" he asked, his voice carrying the weight of his concern for the company's supply chain.

"We are doing everything possible to ensure that our operations remain unaffected," Nick reassured him, though he knew the reality was more complex. "However, we might experience some delays as we tighten our security measures."

He had to be honest about the potential impact, but he also needed to convey that they were in control of the situation.

Then, as he had come to expect, Dr. Haversham, who often asked questions that seemed tangential to the business at hand, raised their hand.

"Nick, while it's good to hear that the breach was contained, I'm curious about something. How do we ensure that our cybersecurity measures don't inadvertently affect the functionality of our components when used in medical equipment? Could a cyber attack on our systems somehow impact the reliability of these parts?"

Dr. Haversham's question, though seemingly peripheral, struck at the heart of the company's reputation for quality and safety.

Nick paused, caught off guard by the question. He took a moment to gather his thoughts, feeling the weight of the board's eyes on him.

"Dr. Haversham, our primary focus is on protecting our internal systems and data," he began, trying to steer the conversation back to the immediate issue.

But Dr. Haversham didn't seem satisfied.

"But what about the broader implications? Could a cyber breach affect the reputation of our components and indirectly affect patient safety through diminished trust in our products?" they pressed, their concern evident in their voice.

For Dr. Haversham, the connection between cybersecurity and patient safety was not just theoretical; it was a critical concern.

Nick felt a flicker of frustration. The question seemed irrelevant to the immediate crisis, but he knew he had to respond thoughtfully.

"That's a good point, Dr. Haversham. Ensuring the integrity of our components is vital, and we have rigorous quality control measures in place to catch any issues. Our focus now is on containment and securing our systems to prevent further breaches," he explained, trying to convey that while the current focus was on the breach, the broader implications were not being ignored.

Dr. Haversham nodded slowly but still seemed lost in thought, clearly not fully grasping the urgency of the situation. Nick made a mental note to delve deeper into this area before the next meeting. He could feel the pressure of not fully addressing Dr. Haversham's concerns and knew he needed to prepare better for such questions in the future.

The board's anxiety was palpable, and Nick realized that his technical explanations were not enough. The meeting continued, but it was clear that the board members were confused and not fully engaged. Nick's update, filled with technical jargon and complex metrics, wasn't resonating with them.

As the meeting concluded, the CEO looked concerned. "Keep us updated on all developments, Nick. We need to be prepared for any fallout."

After the call ended, Nick felt a wave of frustration and anxiety. Despite his best efforts, he couldn't seem to make the board understand the significance of the situation. He knew he needed a better approach.

Feeling a mix of hope and desperation, Nick decided to call Kathy, the experienced CISO he had planned to meet next week. He needed her guidance now more than ever. Dialing her number, he hoped she would pick up despite the short notice.

"Nick, it's good to hear from you," Kathy answered after a few rings. "I heard about the breach. How are you holding up?"

"We're managing, but I need your help. I just updated the board, and it didn't go well. I have to do another update soon, and my usual approach isn't going to cut it. Can you give me some guidance?" Nick asked, desperation creeping into his voice.

"Absolutely," Kathy replied. "The key is to frame your updates in a way that the board can understand and appreciate. You need to connect the technical details to business outcomes. Here's a formulaic approach you can use for your communication:

1. **Identify the Issue**: Clearly state what the problem is.
2. **Immediate Actions Taken**: Explain what has been done so far to address the issue.
3. **Impact on Business**: Describe how the breach impacts business operations, financials, and reputation.
4. **Next Steps**: Outline the steps you plan to take to further mitigate the issue.
5. **Support Needed**: Specify any resources or support you need from the board."

"And remember, your team should handle the technical details. As CISO, you need to stay focused on managing the process and keeping the board informed."

Nick quickly jotted down Kathy's advice. "Got it. Thanks, Kathy. This is exactly what I needed."

"Good luck, Nick. You've got this. Remember, keep it clear and concise, and always link back to how it affects the business."

Nick ended the call, feeling more prepared. He gathered his team for a quick update.

"I've got a better strategy for communicating with the board, thanks to Kathy. She reminded me that you should handle the technical details while I focus on managing the process and updating the board."

Jane nodded. "We've got the technical side covered, Nick. You focus on the board. We've got your back."

Nick smiled, feeling reassured. "Thanks, Jane." He felt a sense of relief knowing his team had it under control.

He quickly revised his update using the framework Kathy provided. He knew he'd be ready for the next Zoom meeting with the board members.

As the board members reappeared on the screen, a couple of hours later, Nick felt more confident.

"Thank you for joining again," he began. "Here's an updated status on the breach using a more business-focused approach,"

1. **Identify the Issue**: "A breach was detected in our customer data systems, leading to unauthorized access to sensitive information."
2. **Immediate Actions Taken**: "Our team has isolated the breach and is focusing on containment. We have increased monitoring and are working on securing all vulnerable systems."
3. **Impact on Business**: "While we've managed to contain the breach, there is potential risk to our reputation and customer trust. Additionally, there might be some delays in operations as we enhance our security measures."
4. **Next Steps**: "We are conducting an internal investigation to determine the scope of the breach and identify the root cause. We will also be implementing additional security protocols to prevent future incidents."
5. **Support Needed**: "To ensure we can fully secure our systems, we may need additional resources and support from all departments. Collaboration will be key in mitigating the impact of this breach."

The board members were pensive but seemed more engaged this time. Mike nodded approvingly.

"Thank you, Nick. This update is much clearer. Keep us informed on any developments."

Kevin added, "And make sure to let us know how we can support you. This is critical for our operations."

The CEO nodded in agreement. "Keep up the good work, Nick. We need to stay on top of this."

As the meeting concluded, Nick felt a sense of relief. The formulaic approach had helped him communicate more effectively. He realized that while the breach was a significant challenge, it was also an opportunity to improve his communication skills and build trust with the board.

Returning to the operations center, Nick felt more confident. He gathered his team for a quick debrief.

"We've made progress containing the breach, but we need to keep the board updated with clear and concise information. Let's continue focusing on securing our systems and be prepared to provide business-focused updates regularly."

His team nodded, and Jane added, "We can handle the technical aspects. You focus on keeping the board informed."

Nick smiled, grateful for his team's support. He knew there was still a long way to go, but with Kathy's guidance and a solid communication strategy, he felt better equipped to navigate the challenges ahead.

Key Takeaways

1. **Effective Communication During a Crisis**: Communicate clearly and calmly during a cybersecurity incident to manage stakeholder expectations and reduce anxiety.
2. **Focus on Broader Implications**: Highlight the financial and reputational impact of cybersecurity incidents, not just the technical details.
3. **Provide Regular Updates**: Keep stakeholders informed with regular updates on the status of the incident and mitigation efforts.
4. **Use a Structured Approach**: Use a formulaic approach to ensure your communication is clear and business focused.
5. **Leverage Expert Guidance**: Seek advice and frameworks from experienced professionals to enhance your communication strategies.

Discussion Prompts

1. How do you currently handle communication during a cybersecurity incident?
2. What strategies can you implement to improve stakeholder communication during a crisis?

3
CHAT WITH THE CEO

Nick stood outside the CEO's office, his stomach in knots. The last board meeting had not gone as well as he had hoped, and he knew the CEO and COO wanted to discuss his performance. He had spent the weekend replaying the meeting in his mind, analyzing every word he had spoken, every slide he had shown, and every question he had failed to answer satisfactorily. The weight of his responsibility as the new CISO bore down on him like never before.

Inside the office, Brian, the CEO, and Sharon, the COO, were already deep in conversation. The atmosphere was serious, and Nick could sense the gravity of the situation even before he entered.

Sharon nodded thoughtfully. "I understand your concerns, Brian, but Nick is new to this role. His technical skills are exceptional, and he has the potential to grow into a great leader. We need to give him the support and guidance he needs to improve."

Brian sighed, rubbing his temples as he considered Sharon's words. "I hope you're right. We can't afford any more missteps. The board needs confidence in our cybersecurity strategy, and that means we need Nick to step up."

Sharon smiled reassuringly, trying to ease Brian's concerns. "He will. I've seen his dedication and willingness to learn. With a bit of guidance and practice, he'll get there. We need to be patient and help him develop those skills."

Brian nodded, though his expression remained serious. "Alright. Let's see how this conversation goes."

At that moment, there was a knock on the door.

"Come in," called Brian, his voice steady but serious.

Nick opened the door and entered, feeling the tension in the room. He saw the serious expressions on Brian and Sharon's faces and felt a knot tighten in his stomach. They motioned for him to sit down.

DOI: 10.1201/9781003597407-3

"Nick, thank you for joining us," Brian began, his tone formal and his expression unreadable. "We wanted to talk to you about your performance during the recent incident."

Nick nodded, his anxiety rising. His mind raced, anticipating the criticism that was about to come. "I understand. It wasn't my best showing," he admitted, trying to keep his voice steady.

Sharon leaned forward, her gaze intense but supportive. "Nick, we know you're capable. Your technical expertise is unquestionable, and your team handled the breach effectively. However, your communication with the board needs improvement."

Brian continued, "The board was left with more questions than answers. We need you to be more concise and connect the technical details to business impacts. The board members are not cybersecurity experts; they need to understand how these incidents affect the company's bottom line and operations."

Nick swallowed, feeling the weight of their words. The feedback stung, but he knew they were right.

"I appreciate the feedback," he began, his voice tinged with frustration at himself. "I did feel that my explanations weren't resonating with them. I've already reached out to Kathy for guidance, and she's given me some valuable advice on how to improve my communication."

Sharon nodded approvingly. "That's a good step, Nick. Kathy's experience will be invaluable. But you also need to practice framing your updates in terms the board can easily grasp. Think about what they care about—financial impacts, operational continuity, and reputation."

Brian added, his tone softer now, "And remember, you're not alone in this. We want to help you succeed. Let's work together to ensure your next presentation is clearer and more impactful."

Nick felt a surge of determination. He knew this was a pivotal moment in his career.

"I understand. I'll focus on framing my updates better and ensuring that I communicate the broader implications of our cybersecurity efforts. I won't let you down."

Sharon smiled slightly, her eyes warm with encouragement. "We know you won't, Nick. Take this as an opportunity to grow. You're a crucial part of our leadership team, and we need you at your best."

Brian stood up, signaling the end of the meeting. "Keep us updated on your progress, and don't hesitate to ask for help if you need it. We're all in this together."

As Nick left the office, he felt a mix of relief and resolve. The conversation had been tough, but it was clear that Brian and Sharon believed in his potential. He knew he had work to do, but with the support of Brian and Sharon, and the guidance from Kathy, he was determined to turn things around. This was his chance to prove himself not just as a technical expert, but as a leader who could effectively communicate and drive the company's cybersecurity strategy forward.

As he walked back to his office, Nick's mind was already racing with ideas. He knew he needed to improve his communication skills, but he also realized that he needed to better understand the board's perspective. What were their biggest concerns? What kept them up at night? He decided that he needed to learn more about the business side of things to really get into the mindset of the board members.

That afternoon, Nick sat down with a stack of business reports and financial statements. He pored over them, trying to understand the company's financials, operational challenges, and strategic goals. The more he read, the more he realized how crucial it was to tie cybersecurity efforts directly to these business objectives. He made notes, jotting down key points that he could use in future presentations.

But Nick knew that reading reports wasn't enough. He recognized that the real challenge wasn't just about understanding the technical details—it was about learning how to communicate them effectively. The more he thought about it, the more he realized that his biggest hurdle was bridging the gap between his technical expertise and the board's business-oriented mindset.

Nick spent the next few days revisiting his notes, reflecting on his recent experiences, and trying to identify where things had gone wrong. He replayed the board meeting in his mind, analyzing each moment when he felt he had lost the board's attention. The more he thought about it, the more he recognized a pattern: he was too focused on the technical details and not enough on the broader business implications.

He began to see that while his knowledge of cybersecurity was solid, his approach to communicating it was not. He was speaking in a language that made sense to him but was foreign to the board members. They needed to understand not just what the cybersecurity measures were, but how they directly impacted the company's financial health, operational efficiency, and reputation.

Nick knew that he couldn't figure this out on his own. He needed guidance from someone who had been through this before, someone who understood both the technical and business sides of cybersecurity. That's when he remembered his upcoming meeting with Kathy. She had a reputation for bridging the gap between technical experts and business leaders, and Nick was hopeful that she could help him do the same.

As he prepared for his meeting with Kathy, Nick felt a mix of anticipation and anxiety. He knew that this meeting could be the turning point he needed, but he also knew that it would require him to step out of his comfort zone and confront his weaknesses head-on. He wasn't ready to present again just yet; there was still much to learn and practice. But he was determined to get there.

In the meantime, Nick made a plan. He would start by listening closely to Kathy, absorbing as much as he could from her experience and insights. He would take her advice to heart and apply it diligently, knowing that his success as a CISO depended on it. As he transitioned from this moment of reflection to his first meeting with Kathy, he felt a renewed sense of determination. The road ahead was challenging, but with the right guidance, he believed he could become the leader his company needed.

Key Takeaways

1. **Seek and Accept Feedback**: Constructive feedback is crucial for growth and improvement.
2. **Focus on Communication**: Frame updates in terms that non-technical stakeholders can understand and relate to.
3. **Collaborate and Seek Support**: Leverage the experience and support of colleagues and mentors to enhance your performance.
4. **Show Determination and Resolve**: Use challenges as opportunities to grow and demonstrate your capabilities.

Discussion Prompts

1. How can you effectively use feedback to improve your performance in a leadership role?
2. What strategies can you implement to ensure your communication is clear and impactful for non-technical stakeholders?
3. How can you leverage the support of your colleagues and mentors to overcome challenges and enhance your leadership skills?

4

BRIDGING THE GAP

The incident was over, and Nick's team had responded effectively. The systems were secure, and the immediate crisis had been managed. But Nick knew that his challenges were far from over. The recent breach had exposed significant gaps in communication between him, his team, and the board.

Nick sat in a quiet corner of a cozy coffee shop, nursing a cup of coffee. He had received a message from Kathy, an experienced CISO from another firm, that she was on her way to discuss his recent challenges. As he looked up, he saw Kathy walking toward him with a friendly smile on her face.

"Nick, it's great to meet you," Kathy said, shaking his hand. "I heard about the breach and the challenges you've been facing. I'm glad I could help."

Nick sighed, feeling a mix of relief and gratitude. "Thank you, Kathy. Your advice was invaluable. Communicating cybersecurity to the board has been more challenging than I expected. I feel like they just don't get it."

Kathy nodded knowingly. "It can be tough. But now that you've made it through the crisis, it's time to focus on advising and guiding the board appropriately moving forward. Let's start with understanding how to bridge the information asymmetry gap."

Nick raised an eyebrow, intrigued but unsure. "Information asymmetry? How can I close that gap?"

Kathy smiled. "Information asymmetry occurs when one party has more information or details about a situation than the other. In our context, it's the disparity between what you, as management, know and what the board knows . This isn't uncommon and occurs in various fields, from banking to mergers and acquisitions [1]. But in cybersecurity, not only is it technical, but it's particularly challenging because often nothing happens, which makes it hard for the board to see the value in what we do [1] [2,22]."

Nick nodded, starting to understand. "So, how do I bridge that gap?"

Kathy pulled out a notepad and began to sketch a diagram. "Think of information asymmetry like this: Good asymmetry is like the relationship between a doctor and a patient or a lawyer and their client. The patient or client trusts the professional to manage the complexities. In this relationship, you want the doctor to know more than you. Bad asymmetry is like dealing with a used car salesman. You're never sure if you're getting the full story, leading to mistrust. In this relationship, you are craving transparency" [5].

Kathy leaned back and continued, "It isn't black and white, though. There is something in the information asymmetry space you should understand called the 'information asymmetry paradox' [5]. While it might seem counterintuitive, having some level of information asymmetry can actually be beneficial. When the board doesn't know all the details, it forces them to ask questions and engage more deeply with the issues. This dynamic can lead to more robust discussions and better decision-making because the board is not passively receiving information but actively seeking to understand it."

She paused, letting the idea sink in before continuing.

"The key is to manage this paradox carefully. You want to provide enough information to ensure the board is well-informed and can make sound decisions, but not so much that they become overwhelmed or complacent. By striking the right balance, you can stimulate engagement and foster a more collaborative environment. This, in turn, can lead to a stronger alignment between the board's strategic goals and our cybersecurity initiatives [5]."

Nick found this perspective enlightening. "So, it's about finding that sweet spot where the board has enough information to be proactive and engaged, without drowning them in details?"

"Exactly," Kathy affirmed. "Think of it as guiding the conversation. Give them the information they need to ask the right questions and see the broader implications. This way, they remain active participants in the decision-making process, which ultimately strengthens their understanding and support of our cybersecurity efforts."

Nick felt a glimmer of hope. Maybe there was a way to bridge the gap after all.

"Alright, I'm willing to give it a try," replied enthusiastically.

"Good," Kathy said. "Now, on the flip side information asymmetry can be particularly problematic in cybersecurity because of non-events. When nothing happens, it can be hard to prove the value of our efforts. The board needs to be informed about existing risks, risks that continue to exist, and emerging threats. They rely on us to keep them abreast of current risks so they can make timely and sound decisions."

"Speaking of risks," Kathy continued, leaning in slightly, "one crucial legal consideration that underscores the importance of keeping the board well-informed is the Caremark standard [12]. Established in the 1996 Caremark decision by the Delaware Supreme Court, this standard holds that directors can be held liable for failing to implement adequate oversight mechanisms, particularly when it comes to risk management. In essence, the Caremark decision highlighted that boards have a duty to ensure that proper information and reporting systems are in place to detect and address risks. This was further solidified by the Stone v. Ritter decision in 2006 [22], where the court emphasized that directors could be liable for failing to act in good faith if they fail to implement such oversight mechanisms or consciously ignore red flags. For CISOs like us, this means we have a critical role in ensuring that the board is not only aware of existing and emerging risks but also understands the potential legal implications of failing to act on this information. Proper communication and documentation of cybersecurity efforts aren't just best practices; they're essential components of fulfilling the board's fiduciary responsibilities under these legal precedents."

Kathy paused for emphasis. "The next step is to apply these risks directly to the business context and answer the 'What's in it for me?' question for each board member. For instance, explain how mitigating a specific risk can prevent potential financial losses, protect our reputation, or ensure operational continuity. Tailoring the information to show the direct impact on their areas of concern helps bridge the gap and makes the abstract risks more tangible and relevant to them [20]. This approach not only closes the information asymmetry but also demonstrates the real value of our cybersecurity efforts in terms they can appreciate and act upon. Always keep the 'What's in it for me?' question at the forefront of your communication strategy."

"That makes a lot of sense," Nick replied, nodding thoughtfully. "I can see how framing the information in terms of their specific concerns would make the risks more relatable and impactful. I'll make sure to connect the dots for them, showing exactly how our efforts directly benefit the business and address their 'What's in it for me?' questions."

Kathy continued, "Cyber insurers face similar issues with adverse selection and moral hazard [21]. Adverse selection is when the board struggles to prioritize risks because they don't have all the information. Moral hazard is when the board can't see the day-to-day actions being taken and may not feel incentivized to support additional cybersecurity measures."

Nick jotted down notes furiously. "Got it. So, it's about making sure they have the right information at the right time."

"Yes," Kathy replied. "We need to implement processes to better understand and communicate the risks in the environment. Regular updates and continuous monitoring are crucial. This not only keeps the board informed but also helps them make better decisions."

Nick paused, thinking about other possible challenges. "Are there other challenges that can cause information asymmetry?"

Kathy leaned back thoughtfully. "Sure. Structural barriers include things like not having enough time to explain ideas thoroughly or not having the right communication channels [3]. Sometimes, your time with the board can be cut short because the previous presenter went over their allotted time. Or you might be scheduled to present right before lunch or at the end of the day when board members are tired or impatient to leave. Hangry boards are impatient, and so are boards that want to go home."

Nick chuckled but knew she was right. "Yeah, I've been there. It can be really tough to get their attention at those times."

"That's why you might also consider meeting one-on-one with executives and board members before the formal meetings," Kathy suggested. "This approach allows you to address their individual concerns and questions directly, building a stronger relationship and trust. When board members feel informed and valued, they're more likely to engage positively in the larger meetings."

Nick looked intrigued. "You mean, like a pre-meeting briefing?"

"Correct!" Kathy said. "These one-on-one sessions give you the chance to tailor your explanations to each person's level of understanding and interest. It's also a great opportunity to build rapport. When they feel they can trust you and rely on you for clear, understandable information, they're more likely to support your initiatives."

Nick felt a renewed sense of determination. "Thanks, Kathy. This is really helpful."

Kathy continued, "Another aspect to consider is the different types of information you share. You need to be strategic about what and how you communicate. For example, boards often struggle with non-observable aspects of cybersecurity – the idea that nothing happened because your measures are working. This can make it hard for them to see the value in ongoing investments. You need to emphasize the potential risks and the importance of preventive measures. It's not just about what has happened, but what could happen if these measures aren't in place."

Nick thought about this for a moment. "So, I need to paint a picture of both the current state and the potential future without our cybersecurity measures?"

"Now you're getting it," Kathy said. "Use scenarios and case studies from other companies if needed. Show them what can go wrong without proper cybersecurity. Highlight the importance of proactive measures rather than reactive responses but stay away from FUD."

Kathy paused again before adding, "And don't forget about the language you use. Technical jargon can alienate your audience. You need to translate technical details into business language. Talk in terms of financial impact, operational efficiency, and reputational risk. This will make your message more relatable and easier to understand."

Nick nodded, jotting down more notes. "Got it. I need to focus on business impacts and use language they can relate to."

"Yes," Kathy said. "And always be prepared to answer their questions. The more transparent you are, the more trust you'll build. Remember, they need to feel confident that you're managing the cybersecurity risks effectively. And if you don't know the answer to something, be honest about it—let them know you'll look it up and get back to them. I call that taking a look-up, and it shows integrity and a commitment to providing them with accurate information."

Nick felt a surge of motivation. "This is incredibly helpful, Kathy. I feel like I have a much better grasp on how to communicate effectively with the board."

Kathy nodded. "Remember, Nick, the way we present information can significantly influence how it is received and acted upon. Reducing the information asymmetry by framing information in relatable and clear terms is key. And always be prepared for follow-up questions and discussions to further clarify any concerns."

Kathy noticed Nick's thoughtful expression and leaned in slightly. "You know, Nick, one of the things I've found most helpful is adopting a storytelling approach. When you share technical details with the board, don't just list facts—tell a story. Frame the cybersecurity incidents as narratives with a beginning, middle, and end. Explain the threat as the antagonist, the response as the plot, and the resolution as the victory. This way, the board can follow the progression and see the impact of your actions in a more relatable way."

Nick's eyes lit up. "That makes a lot of sense. People remember stories, not just data points."

"Exactly," Kathy said with a smile. "You can also use this approach when discussing potential risks. Create a scenario that's relevant to the business—something that could plausibly happen if the cybersecurity measures aren't in place. This makes the risks tangible, and it helps the board understand why investing in cybersecurity is essential."

Nick was already thinking about how he could apply this in his next presentation. "I could frame our recent breach as a story, showing how we identified the villain, responded to the threat, and ultimately secured the company's assets. And for future risks, I could use hypothetical scenarios that directly tie into our business operations."

Kathy nodded. "That's the idea. The more you can engage them with a story, the more likely they are to grasp the importance of what you're doing. It also makes the information stick, which is crucial when you're asking them to support new initiatives or approve budgets."

Nick took a deep breath, feeling more optimistic. "This is a lot to think about, but it's really helpful. I'm starting to see how I can bridge that gap."

"Good," Kathy said encouragingly. "And remember, Nick, it's not just about the board meetings. The way you communicate with your team and other stakeholders is equally important. If they see you struggling to communicate with the board, they might lose confidence in your leadership. But if you can demonstrate clear, effective communication, it will inspire confidence across the board—literally and figuratively."

Nick smiled, appreciating the play on words. "You're right. I need to lead by example, not just in the technical aspects but in how I communicate and interact with everyone involved."

Kathy gave him a reassuring pat on the back. "You've got this, Nick. It's a learning curve, but you're already making great progress. Keep refining your approach, and don't hesitate to reach out if you need more guidance."

Nick nodded, feeling a renewed sense of determination. "Thanks, Kathy. I really appreciate all your help. I'll keep working on this and make sure I'm ready for the next board meeting—and for anything else that comes my way."

Kathy smiled warmly. "I have no doubt you'll succeed, Nick. Just remember that communication is a skill, and like any skill, it takes practice and refinement. You're on the right path, and I'm confident you'll become the kind of CISO who not only understands cybersecurity but also knows how to lead, communicate, and inspire."

As they wrapped up their meeting, Nick felt a deep sense of gratitude for Kathy's mentorship. He knew that the journey ahead would be challenging, but with her guidance and his newfound insights, he was ready to take on the role of a truly effective CISO.

Back at the office, Nick immediately began implementing Kathy's advice. He started by revising his communication strategy, focusing on the key points Kathy had emphasized: storytelling, connecting technical details to business outcomes, and managing information asymmetry. He also made a point to schedule one-on-one meetings with board members before the next big presentation, just as Kathy had suggested.

As Nick worked late into the evening, preparing his next presentation, he felt more confident than he had in weeks. He knew that his technical expertise was strong, but now he also had the tools to communicate that expertise in a way that resonated with the board. For the first time, he felt like he was truly on the path to becoming the leader his company needed.

He realized that while the recent breach had been a significant challenge, it had also been a valuable learning experience. It had forced him to confront his weaknesses and seek out the guidance he needed to grow. And in doing so, it had set him on a course toward becoming not just a CISO but a trusted and effective leader.

As he saved the latest version of his presentation and closed his laptop, Nick knew that the hard work was just beginning. But with Kathy's advice and his own determination, he was confident that he could rise to the challenge. The journey ahead would require patience, practice, and perseverance, but he was ready to take it on.

Nick glanced at the clock and decided to call it a night. He knew that tomorrow would bring new challenges, but he also knew that he was better equipped to face them. As he headed out of the office, he felt a renewed sense of purpose and determination. This was just the beginning, and he was ready to take the next step in his journey as a CISO.

Key Takeaways

1. **Understand Information Asymmetry**: Recognize the disparity in information between management and the board, and work to bridge this gap.
2. **Information Asymmetry Paradox**: Some level of information asymmetry can be beneficial, as it encourages board members to ask questions and engage more deeply.
3. **Use Relatable Analogies**: Simplify complex concepts with analogies that make sense to non-technical stakeholders.
4. **Speak Plainly**: Avoid technical jargon and explain cybersecurity measures in terms that highlight their business relevance.
5. **Meet One-on-One**: Consider pre-meeting briefings with key stakeholders to address their specific concerns and build trust.
6. **Highlight Preventive Measures**: Emphasize the importance of proactive cybersecurity measures to prevent potential threats.

Discussion Prompts

1. How can you use one-on-one meetings with board members to improve their understanding of cybersecurity risks?
2. What strategies can you implement to ensure your cybersecurity presentations are relatable and easily understood by non-technical stakeholders?

5

OVERCOMING EMOTIONS

Nick was feeling more confident about his next steps in bridging the information asymmetry gap with the board. He was already preparing for his next meeting with Kathy, eager to dive into another critical area she had mentioned: the affect heuristic. Kathy had explained that people often react emotionally to cybersecurity threats because they don't fully understand them, which can lead to fear and poor decision-making.

Nick arrived at the coffee shop early, armed with a notebook full of questions and notes from his recent research. As he sipped his coffee, he reviewed his notes, eager to absorb more insights from Kathy.

A few minutes later, Kathy walked in, her usual confident smile lighting up the room.

"Good to see you again, Nick," she said, taking a seat across from him. "Ready to tackle the next challenge?"

"Absolutely," Nick replied. "I've been reading up on the affect heuristic and how emotions can impact decision-making. It's fascinating, but I'm still trying to figure out how to apply it to our board communications."

Kathy nodded. "The affect heuristic is a powerful concept. It refers to the way people rely on their emotions and gut feelings to make decisions, especially under conditions of uncertainty [10]. When it comes to cybersecurity, the fear of the unknown can often lead to negative reactions and hasty decisions."

Kathy continued, "For example, after a high-profile data breach, executives and board members might push for immediate, sweeping changes to the security management and/or infrastructure out of fear, without fully understanding the implications or effectiveness of those changes. This reaction can lead to wasted resources or even increased vulnerabilities because the decisions are based on an emotional response rather than a thorough risk assessment [8]."

DOI: 10.1201/9781003597407-5

Nick nodded, recalling the research he had studied. "Yes, I remember reading about that. Decision-makers often resort to emotional shortcuts in the face of cybersecurity threats. They prioritize actions that seem to offer immediate relief over those that are strategically sound [23]. It's a classic case of the affect heuristic at work."

Kathy smiled. "Spot on. When people are scared, they tend to choose options that provide a sense of security and familiarity, even if those options aren't the best long-term solutions. It's our job to present information in a way that reduces this emotional bias. We need to provide clear, rational explanations and show how our strategies are designed to protect the company in a more effective, sustainable way."

Kathy went on, "Failure to communicate risks effectively can lead to inappropriate decisions by executives and boards [25]. Emotions influenced by the environment, past experiences, and reactions impact decision-making. People often prefer simple comparisons of good and bad feelings over complex thoughts. This means that negative or positive moods can significantly influence their behavior and decisions. In cybersecurity, when board members are emotionally driven by fear, it clouds their judgment and leads to suboptimal decisions."

"That makes sense," Nick said. "So, how do we overcome that?"

Kathy smiled. "The key is to present information in a way that reduces fear and promotes rational thinking. Here are some strategies to consider:

1. **Use Relatable Examples**: Analogies and stories can help demystify complex cybersecurity issues. For instance, compare cybersecurity measures to home security systems. Just as people install locks and alarms to protect their homes, companies need similar measures to protect their digital assets.

2. **Avoid Technical Jargon**: Speak in plain language. Technical terms can be intimidating and confusing, leading to fear and misunderstanding. Translate technical details into business terms and explain their relevance to the company's goals.

3. **Highlight Positive Outcomes**: Focus on the successes and preventive measures that have protected the company from potential threats. This can build confidence and reduce anxiety about future risks.

4. **Show the Bigger Picture**: Connect cybersecurity efforts to the overall health and success of the business. Explain how these measures support operational efficiency, financial stability, and customer trust.

5. **Engage in Dialogue**: Encourage questions and provide clear, straightforward answers. This builds trust and helps the board feel more informed and less fearful."

Nick scribbled down the strategies, feeling more optimistic. "That sounds like a solid approach. Can you give me an example of how you've applied these strategies in your own board presentations?"

Kathy leaned back, thinking for a moment. "Sure. In one of my previous roles, we had a major phishing attack that nearly compromised our customer database. Instead of focusing on the technical details of how we stopped it, I framed the discussion around the potential business impact if we hadn't intervened."

"I used a simple analogy: 'Imagine our customer database is like a vault filled with gold. A phishing attack is like a thief trying to pick the lock. Our cybersecurity measures are the high-tech security system that detects and stops the thief before they can steal anything.' This helped the board understand the importance of our efforts without getting lost in the technicalities."

Nick nodded, finding the analogy effective. "I see how that can make a big difference. It makes the threat more tangible and the response more relatable."

"Right," Kathy said. "And by highlighting how we prevented a potential crisis, I was able to shift the focus from fear to proactive success. This not only eased their concerns but also reinforced the value of our cybersecurity investments."

Nick felt inspired. "I think I can apply these principles to our next board meeting. But what about handling negative emotions that might already exist, like frustration or distrust?"

"Good question," Kathy replied. "Address those emotions directly. Acknowledge the board's concerns and show empathy. For example, if they're frustrated about past incidents, assure them that you've learned from those experiences and are implementing stronger measures. Transparency and honesty go a long way in building trust."

Nick nodded, taking detailed notes. "Got it. I'll make sure to incorporate these strategies. It's about creating a narrative that resonates emotionally while still being grounded in facts."

"Precisely," Kathy said. "And remember, you're not just presenting information—you're telling a story that connects with your audience on a deeper level. You want to answer their internal 'What's in it for me?' question. When they understand and trust your story, they're more likely to support your initiatives."

Nick leaned forward, eager to dive deeper into the topic. "I've read that the affect heuristic means people make decisions based on their emotions and past experiences, rather than rational calculations. How does this apply to the board?"

Kathy nodded, "The affect heuristic is when a person selects courses of action using emotions influenced by the stimulus of the environment, experience, and reactions. Affect serves as a source of information impacting the decision or judgment being made, and these feelings are impacted by prior experiences [17]. For example, if a board member had a negative experience with a cybersecurity incident in the past, that emotion could heavily influence their current decision-making."

Nick considered this. "So, if they have had a bad experience, they might overestimate the risks or react more strongly than necessary?"

"Yes, that's right," Kathy said. "And it can also go the other way. If they haven't experienced a cyber threat directly, they might underestimate the risks. It's our job to balance these emotional reactions with clear, factual information. Research shows that affect influences information processing and behavior. A negative or positive mood can motivate their behavior and decision-making [17]. So, we need to manage these moods by presenting information in a way that is clear, understandable, and relevant to them."

Kathy continued, "Research has found that the affect heuristic is particularly applicable in cybersecurity. This means that emotions often come into play when the board or executives make poor decisions without good information. For instance, in a flood scenario, people often use the affect heuristic rather than rational calculation to react to risk situations. This biological response is a fight-or-flight mechanism [15]. When faced with immediate danger, our brains are wired to prioritize quick, emotional reactions over slow, rational thinking. This can be useful in genuinely life-threatening situations but is problematic when applied to complex issues like cybersecurity."

Nick jotted down more notes. "That makes sense. How do we help them move past these emotional reactions to make better decisions?"

Kathy smiled. "One technique is to present the risks in terms that the executives and board will understand. For example, presenting the likelihood of a cyber attack as either a probability or frequency. Studies show that presenting risks in a 1-in-X format can be perceived as higher than when presented as a probability [25]. Also, making the risk personally relevant can increase its perceived impact. When board members feel that the risk directly affects them or their responsibilities, answering the 'What's in it for me?', they are more likely to take it seriously."

Nick nodded, feeling the pieces fall into place. "So, it's about making the risks relatable and understandable, and framing them in a way that prompts rational rather than emotional responses."

"Yes, you're getting it," Kathy said. "And it's important to remember that people always have feelings; a truly neutral affective state is rare [9]. When people feel neutral, it's often because the information presented doesn't seem relevant or is sufficiently understood. Our job is to ensure that cybersecurity is seen as relevant and understandable, which will naturally elicit an appropriate level of attention and concern."

Nick felt a surge of motivation. "This is incredibly helpful, Kathy. I feel like I have a much better grasp on how to communicate effectively with the board."

Kathy nodded. "Remember, Nick, the way we present information can significantly influence how it is received and acted upon. Reducing the affect heuristic by framing information in relatable and clear terms is key. And always be prepared for follow-up questions and discussions to further clarify any concerns."

As their meeting wrapped up, Nick thanked Kathy for her invaluable insights and promised to keep her updated on his progress. He felt more equipped than ever to handle the emotional and psychological aspects of communicating cybersecurity risks to the board.

Back at the office, Nick began preparing his strategies for future board interactions. He drafted potential scenarios and responses, focusing on clear, relatable language and real-world analogies. He knew that each board member brought their own experiences, biases, and emotional triggers to the table—factors that could significantly influence their decision-making. To counteract the affect heuristic, Nick planned to weave in examples that would resonate with their past experiences, helping them see cybersecurity through a more informed and rational lens.

Nick also recognized the importance of addressing the information asymmetry gap that often clouded these discussions. The board relied on him to filter complex technical details into actionable insights, but this process was more than just simplifying information. It required him to be a guide, helping them construct their understanding based on their existing knowledge while bridging the gaps that could lead to misconceptions or fear-driven decisions. To achieve this, Nick decided to adopt a more constructivist approach, encouraging active participation and dialogue during his presentations. He would ask probing questions that prompted board members to connect new information with what they already knew, fostering a deeper understanding of the issues at hand.

In line with this approach, Nick planned to schedule more one-on-one pre-meetings with key board members and executives. These meetings would serve as opportunities to tailor his message to each individual's concerns and level of understanding. By engaging them in discussions that were relevant to their roles, Nick could help them build a more robust mental framework for evaluating cybersecurity risks. He aimed to transform these interactions into collaborative learning experiences, where board members felt empowered to ask questions and express their concerns, knowing that he would guide them toward the right conclusions.

Nick was confident that these efforts would pay off. By bridging the affect heuristic and closing the information asymmetry gap, he was laying the groundwork for a more informed and engaged board. He was moving beyond simply delivering information to facilitating a process of shared understanding—one that would lead to better decision-making and stronger support for his cybersecurity initiatives.

The journey was still ahead of him, but Nick felt more prepared to face the challenges that lay ahead. He understood that this was not just about the next board meeting, but about building a long-term relationship of trust and mutual respect. By adopting an approach that blended technical expertise with an understanding of human psychology and adult learning principles, Nick was on his way to becoming a more effective CISO and a trusted advisor to the board.

Key Takeaways

1. **Understand the Affect Heuristic**: Recognize that emotions can heavily influence decision-making, especially in areas like cybersecurity.
2. **Use Relatable Analogies**: Simplify complex concepts with analogies that make sense to non-technical stakeholders.
3. **Speak Plainly**: Avoid technical jargon and explain cybersecurity measures in terms that highlight their business relevance.
4. **Highlight Successes**: Focus on positive outcomes and how preventive measures have protected the company.
5. **Engage and Empathize**: Address board members' emotions directly, showing empathy and building trust through transparency.

Discussion Prompts

1. How can you use relatable analogies to explain complex cybersecurity concepts to non-technical stakeholders?
2. What strategies can you implement to address and reduce the negative emotions associated with cybersecurity discussions?
3. How can you balance acknowledging emotional concerns with promoting evidence-based decision-making in cybersecurity?

Nick felt more confident about bridging the information asymmetry gap and managing the affect heuristic when communicating with the board. But there was another critical piece of advice Kathy had hinted at: building trust by reducing self-orientation. He knew that building trust was fundamental to ensuring the board felt secure in its decision-making.

Nick arrived at the coffee shop once more, this time with a clearer idea of what he needed to learn. As Kathy joined him, he greeted her warmly and got straight to the point.

"Kathy, thanks again for meeting with me. I've been thinking a lot about how to build trust with the board, and you mentioned reducing self-orientation. Can you explain that in more detail?"

Kathy smiled, appreciating Nick's direct approach. "Of course, Nick. Trust is built on four key elements: credibility, reliability, intimacy, and self-orientation [14]. Credibility is about your expertise and credentials. Reliability is about your consistency in delivering what you promise. Intimacy is about the emotional closeness and safety people feel with you. And self-orientation is about whose interests you are focused on—yours or theirs."

Nick nodded, taking notes. "So, reducing self-orientation means focusing more on their needs and less on promoting myself?"

"Exactly," Kathy said. "Let me explain further using the trust equation. The trust equation is:

$$Trust = \frac{Credibility + Reliability + Initimacy}{Self\ Orientation}$$

This equation highlights that while credibility, reliability, and intimacy are crucial, the impact of self-orientation is significant because it's in the denominator. The lower your self-orientation—meaning the more you focus on others rather than yourself—the higher the trust.

DOI: 10.1201/9781003597407-6   **37**

It's just math. If your self-orientation is high, it diminishes the trust you've built through credibility, reliability, and intimacy."

Nick leaned in, clearly understanding the math behind it. "So, even if I'm highly credible, reliable, and have a good relationship with them, if they sense that I'm more focused on my own interests, it will reduce their trust in me?"

"Exactly," Kathy affirmed. "You need to show the board that you are genuinely concerned with their needs and the organization's well-being. When they feel that your primary focus is on them and not on showcasing your own achievements, trust naturally builds."

Kathy, sensing an opportunity to introduce another crucial concept. "Nick, there's another element at play here, that we need to cover, that you might not have considered—how adults learn. Board members aren't just looking for information; they need it presented in a way that aligns with how they absorb and apply knowledge. Adult learning theory, or andragogy, tells us that people learn best when information is relevant to their needs, immediately applicable, and problem-centered [16]. If you approach these discussions like a classroom lecture full of abstract technical details, you'll lose them. But if you frame security in terms of real-world business impact, decision-making, and strategic outcomes, they'll engage. Think of it this way, you're not just informing them—you're teaching them in a way that helps them act.

Nick, eager to dive deeper. "This is great to keep in mind. With that, can you give me some practical examples of how I can reduce self-orientation in my interactions with the board while keeping it relevant and practical?"

"Sure," Kathy replied. "Here are a few strategies:

- **Listen Actively**: Pay close attention to what the board members are saying. Show that you value their input by responding thoughtfully and incorporating their feedback into your plans.
- **Ask Questions**: Instead of always presenting your solutions, ask the board members about their concerns and what they think are the priorities. This shows that you respect their perspective and are open to their ideas.

- **Empathize**: Put yourself in their shoes. Understand their pressures, challenges, and what success looks like from their viewpoint. This helps you communicate in a way that resonates with their experiences and priorities.
- **Provide Value**: Focus on how your actions and decisions benefit the organization and the board members. Highlight the positive impacts on business goals, financial health, and operational efficiency rather than just technical accomplishments.
- **Be Transparent**: Share both the successes and the challenges. When things don't go as planned, be honest about what happened and what you're doing to address it. Transparency builds trust because it shows you're not hiding anything."

Nick jotted down the strategies, feeling more equipped. "That makes sense. How do I balance being transparent about challenges without causing panic or losing their confidence?"

Kathy nodded. "Great question. It's all about framing. When discussing challenges, always pair them with solutions. For example, if you're reporting on a security vulnerability, explain what measures you're taking to mitigate the risk and how you plan to prevent similar issues in the future. This shows that you're proactive and solutions-oriented, which builds confidence rather than fear."

Nick was intrigued. "Framing sounds like a great psychological technique. Can you expand on how framing works and why it's effective?"

"Absolutely," Kathy said. "Framing is about presenting information in a way that influences perception and decision-making [6]. It's a powerful technique in psychology because it helps shape the way people interpret information. When you frame a message, you're highlighting certain aspects while downplaying others to guide the audience toward a desired conclusion. In the context of cybersecurity, effective framing can reduce fear and encourage a more rational, confident approach."

"Ah, tying in the affect heuristic," Nick noted.

"Right," Kathy continued. "For instance, instead of saying, 'We discovered a major security vulnerability,' you could frame it as, 'We identified an area for improvement in our security systems and are implementing measures to enhance our defenses.' This positive framing focuses on the proactive steps being taken rather than the problem itself, which can reduce anxiety and build confidence."

Nick nodded, seeing the value in this approach. "So, it's about highlighting the positive actions and solutions rather than dwelling on the negative aspects?"

"Yes," Kathy replied. "Framing can also help in making abstract concepts more concrete. For example, instead of talking about potential data breaches, you could frame it as protecting our customers' personal information. This makes the issue more relatable and emphasizes the importance of cybersecurity in a context that board members care about."

Nick nodded. "I see the value in that. But what about board members like Dr. Haversham? They often ask questions that seem off-topic or not directly related to the business implications."

Kathy smiled. "Dr. Haversham's questions might seem irrelevant at first, but they're often rooted in genuine concern. The key is to redirect their focus in a way that addresses their underlying worries while still keeping the conversation productive."

Nick looked curious. "Can you give me an example?"

"Sure," Kathy said. "Let's say Dr. Haversham asks about the potential impact of a data breach on patient safety, even though our company doesn't deal directly with patients. You could frame your response to align with their concerns while keeping it relevant to the business."

Nick leaned in, ready to take notes. Kathy continued. "You might say something like, 'Dr. Haversham, while our company doesn't directly handle patient care, protecting our customers' personal information is crucial. A data breach could lead to significant harm, such as identity theft, which can affect our customers' lives profoundly. By ensuring robust cybersecurity measures, we're safeguarding our customers' trust and well-being, much like how patient safety is paramount in healthcare.'"

Nick jotted down the example, appreciating the practical approach. "So, the idea is to connect his concerns with the broader impact on our customers and the business."

"Right," Kathy affirmed. "By framing your response this way, you acknowledge his concerns and show how they tie into the company's objectives. This builds trust because it demonstrates that you're listening and addressing what matters to him while still keeping the focus on the business."

Nick thought for a moment. "What if they ask about something completely out of left field, like the potential environmental impact of our cybersecurity measures?"

Kathy chuckled. "In that case, you can still use framing to guide the conversation. For example, you could say, 'Dr. Haversham, that's an interesting point. While our cybersecurity measures themselves don't directly impact the environment, ensuring our systems are secure helps prevent data breaches, which can have far-reaching consequences, including economic and social impacts. By protecting our company and our customers, we're contributing to a more stable and responsible business environment.'"

Nick smiled, feeling more confident. "I think I'm getting the hang of this. It's about finding the common ground and making the connections clear."

"Exactly," Kathy said. "Framing is a powerful tool. It helps make abstract concepts concrete and relevant to your audience. By addressing their concerns and showing the broader implications, you build trust and ensure your message resonates."

Nick leaned back, processing the information. "Got it. So, by framing the information in a positive and relatable way, I can help the board feel more secure and confident in our cybersecurity measures."

"Precisely," Kathy said. "And remember, framing isn't about misleading or sugar-coating the truth. It's about presenting the facts in a way that highlights your proactive approach and the value of your actions. This builds trust and reassures the board that you have things under control."

Nick smiled, feeling a renewed sense of purpose. "Thanks, Kathy. This has been incredibly helpful. I feel like I have a much clearer path forward."

Kathy returned his smile. "I'm glad to hear that, Nick. Remember, building trust is a continuous process. Keep focusing on their needs, and you'll see the difference in how they respond to you."

As their meeting wrapped up, Nick felt a surge of motivation. He knew that by reducing self-orientation and focusing on the board's needs, he could build stronger relationships and become a more effective CISO.

Back at the office, Nick began implementing the strategies Kathy had shared. He scheduled one-on-one meetings with key board members to better understand their concerns and priorities. During these meetings, he listened actively, asked insightful questions, and empathized with their challenges.

Nick also made sure to be transparent in his communications, sharing both successes and challenges with a focus on how he was addressing any issues. He highlighted the positive impacts of his cybersecurity initiatives on the business, making the connection between technical measures and business outcomes clear.

As he prepared for the next board meeting, Nick felt more confident and prepared. He knew that by reducing self-orientation and focusing on building trust, he was not only improving his communication but also strengthening the board's confidence in his leadership.

Key Takeaways

1. **Build Trust**: Trust is built on credibility, reliability, intimacy, and reducing self-orientation.
2. **Trust Equation**: Understanding the trust equation helps emphasize the importance of reducing self-orientation.
3. **Listen Actively**: Show that you value the board members' input by listening and responding thoughtfully.
4. **Ask Questions**: Engage the board members by asking about their concerns and priorities.
5. **Empathize**: Understand the board members' perspectives and communicate in a way that resonates with their experiences.
6. **Be Transparent**: Share both successes and challenges with solutions to build confidence and trust.
7. **Use Framing**: Present information in a way that highlights positive actions and solutions to build confidence and reduce fear.

Discussion Prompts

1. How can you reduce self-orientation in your interactions with stakeholders to build trust?

2. What strategies can you implement to ensure your communications are transparent and solutions-oriented?
3. How can you use framing to present information in a way that builds confidence and reduces fear?

7

BUSINESS LANGUAGE

Nick's confidence in communicating with the board was growing, thanks to Kathy's invaluable advice on information asymmetry, the affect heuristic, and building trust by reducing self-orientation. However, he knew there was another critical aspect to effective communication: understanding his audience. Kathy had emphasized that the language of business is the language the audience understands, so knowing the audience is key.

Nick arrived at the coffee shop once more, eager to dive into the next topic. Kathy joined him shortly, and after their usual greetings, they got straight to business.

"Kathy, you've mentioned before that understanding the audience is crucial. Can we dive deeper into that? How do I ensure I'm speaking their language?" Nick asked.

Kathy nodded. "Absolutely, Nick. Understanding your audience is about knowing their priorities, pressures, and what drives their decisions. Each board member might have different concerns based on their roles and experiences, like Dr. Haversham. To communicate effectively, you need to tailor your message to address those specific concerns [2]."

Nick laughed. "Haversham," leaned forward, ready to take notes. "That makes sense. How do I go about understanding their concerns better?"

"Start by researching each board member," Kathy suggested. "Learn about their backgrounds, their current roles, and any past experiences that might influence their perspective on cybersecurity. For example, a CFO might be primarily concerned with financial impacts, while a COO might focus on operational disruptions [18]. Knowing these details helps you frame your message in a way that resonates with them."

DOI: 10.1201/9781003597407-7

Nick jotted down the advice, thinking about how he could apply it. "So, I need to frame my communication differently for each board member based on their role and concerns?"

"Exactly," Kathy said. "Let's break it down further. Here are some steps to help you understand and communicate effectively with your audience:

1. **Research Their Backgrounds**: Understand their professional histories, expertise, and any previous roles that might influence their current concerns.

2. **Identify Their Priorities**: Determine what matters most to each board member. Is it financial stability, operational efficiency, compliance, customer satisfaction, or something else?

3. **Listen and Observe**: Pay attention during meetings to what each board member emphasizes. What questions do they ask? What issues do they seem most concerned about?

4. **Engage in One-on-One Conversations**: As we discussed before, meeting with board members individually can provide valuable insights into their specific concerns and priorities. Use these meetings to ask open-ended questions and listen actively. One-on-one conversations also provide them an opportunity to ask questions openly without the pressure of their peers.

5. **Tailor Your Message**: Customize your communication to highlight how cybersecurity impacts their areas of concern. For example, for the CFO, focus on the financial implications of a data breach and the cost savings of preventive measures. For the COO, emphasize the importance of maintaining operational continuity and avoiding disruptions. But remember to bring it all together for the audience as a whole.

6. **Use Relatable Analogies and Examples**: Frame your message in terms that are familiar to them. Use analogies that relate to their field. For instance, compare cybersecurity to financial audits for the CFO, or to supply chain logistics for the COO, and to patient care for the medical professionals in the room.

7. **Provide Clear, Actionable Information**: Be specific about what actions are needed and how they will address the board members' concerns. Avoid vague statements and focus on tangible outcomes."

Nick nodded, taking in the detailed steps. "This is really helpful, Kathy. Can you give me an example of how you've tailored your communication to different board members in the past?"

"Of course," Kathy said. "In one of my previous roles, we had a diverse board with varying concerns. The CFO was always focused on the financial impact, so I framed cybersecurity investments as a way to prevent costly breaches and avoid regulatory fines. I used concrete numbers to show potential savings and return on investment."

"For the COO, I highlighted how cybersecurity measures ensured operational continuity and minimized downtime. I shared examples of other companies that suffered operational disruptions due to cyberattacks and how our preventive measures could help avoid such scenarios."

"For the head of HR, I emphasized the importance of protecting employee data and maintaining trust within the organization. I discussed the potential impact on employee morale and the company's reputation if personal data were compromised."

Nick could see how this tailored approach would be effective. "So, it's about connecting cybersecurity to what each board member cares about most."

"Exactly," Kathy replied. "Answer their internal, 'What's in it for me?' When they see that you understand their priorities and are addressing their specific concerns, they're more likely to trust your recommendations and support your initiatives."

Nick felt a surge of motivation. "I can definitely do that. I'll start by scheduling one-on-one meetings and doing my research on each board member."

"That's a great plan," Kathy said. "And remember, this isn't a one-time effort. Continuously engaging with the board members and understanding their evolving concerns is key to maintaining effective communication."

Nick paused, reflecting on the advice Kathy had just given him. "You know, this reminds me of something I've read about in adult learning theory—specifically, andragogy, which is the method and practice of teaching adult learners. It's about understanding that adults bring their own experiences and knowledge to the table, and they learn best when they can see the direct relevance of what they're being taught to their own lives [19]."

Kathy's eyes lit up with interest. "That's an excellent point, Nick. Andragogy really ties into what we've been discussing. When you're communicating with the board, you're essentially teaching them about cybersecurity in a way that's relevant to their experiences and concerns. You're not just giving them information; you're helping them learn how that information impacts their roles and the organization as a whole."

"Exactly," Nick agreed. "And it's also about respecting their need to be involved in the learning process. When I engage them in one-on-one conversations and tailor my message to their concerns, I'm not just telling them what they need to know—I'm involving them in the process, making it a two-way conversation. This way, they feel more ownership over the decisions that are made, and they're more likely to support the initiatives I propose."

Kathy smiled. "And that's where the constructivist approach comes in. It's about building knowledge together, constructing a shared understanding of the challenges and how to address them. By taking this approach, you're not just delivering a presentation; you're facilitating a dialogue where everyone contributes to the solution. This collaborative process is key to effective communication and decision-making at the board level."

Nick felt a renewed sense of purpose. "So, it's not just about me delivering information—it's about creating an environment where we can all build on each other's knowledge and experience. That makes so much sense, especially in the context of cybersecurity, where the landscape is always changing and there's always something new to learn."

Kathy nodded. "Exactly. And by framing your communication in this way, you're not only helping the board understand the technical aspects of cybersecurity, but you're also empowering them to make informed decisions that align with the organization's goals. It's about creating a partnership where everyone is working together toward the same objectives."

Nick thanked Kathy for her insights and left the meeting feeling more prepared than ever. He spent the next few days researching each board member's background, identifying their priorities, and preparing tailored communication strategies for his upcoming meetings.

As he refined his strategies, Nick also decided to keep a journal of his observations and interactions. This would help him track patterns in the board members' concerns and improve his ability to tailor his communications. He knew that the process of understanding his audience would be ongoing, but he was committed to getting it right.

Nick felt a growing sense of clarity about how he could become not just a presenter of information, but a trusted advisor who truly understood and aligned with the board's needs. He knew that this approach would take time and effort, but he was ready for the challenge. By building on the foundation of trust, empathy, and tailored communication, Nick was confident that he was on the right path to becoming a more effective CISO.

Key Takeaways

1. **Know Your Audience**: Understand the backgrounds, priorities, and concerns of each board member.
2. **Tailor Your Message**: Customize your communication to address the specific concerns of each board member.
3. **Engage in One-on-One Conversations**: Use individual meetings to gain deeper insights into their perspectives.
4. **Use Relatable Analogies**: Frame cybersecurity in terms that resonate with each board member's field of expertise.
5. **Provide Clear, Actionable Information**: Focus on tangible outcomes and specific actions that address their concerns.

Discussion Prompts

1. How can you better understand the priorities and concerns of your stakeholders?
2. What strategies can you use to tailor your communication to different audience members?

8

ONE-ON-ONE MEETINGS

Nick decided to take Kathy's advice and meet with the board members one-on-one. He believed that understanding their individual concerns would help him communicate more effectively during the board meetings.

Meeting with Mike

Nick sat across from Mike, the former CFO and current board member, in Mike's spacious office. The walls were lined with awards and certificates, showcasing his financial expertise.

"Mike, thanks for taking the time to meet with me," Nick began. "I wanted to get a better understanding of your concerns regarding our cybersecurity efforts."

Mike leaned back in his chair, his expression thoughtful. "Nick, my main concern is how cybersecurity impacts our financial stability. I need to understand the costs involved and how these measures protect our bottom line."

Nick nodded. "I understand. Cybersecurity can seem like a cost center, but it's an investment in protecting our financial assets. For instance, a data breach can lead to significant financial losses, not just from direct theft but also from legal fees, fines, and loss of customer trust. By investing in robust cybersecurity measures, we're actually safeguarding our financial health."

Mike's eyes narrowed as he considered Nick's words. "So, you're saying it's about risk management and cost avoidance?"

"Exactly," Nick replied. "By preventing breaches, we're avoiding the potentially massive costs associated with them. It's about protecting our revenue and ensuring long-term financial stability. But there's more to it than just prevention. A robust security program can also set us apart from our competitors and give us a competitive advantage."

DOI: 10.1201/9781003597407-8

Mike raised an eyebrow, intrigued. "How so?"

Nick leaned forward, eager to explain. "Think about it this way: if we can demonstrate to our customers and partners that we have top-notch cybersecurity, it builds trust and confidence in our brand. Customers are increasingly concerned about their data privacy and security. If we can assure them that their information is safe with us, it can be a significant selling point. Additionally, our strong cybersecurity posture can make us a more attractive partner for other businesses, leading to new opportunities and partnerships."

Mike tapped his fingers on the desk thoughtfully. "But what about the return on investment for these cybersecurity measures? How do we quantify the value they bring compared to their cost?"

Nick anticipated this question and was ready with an answer. "That's a great question, Mike. One way to quantify the ROI is by calculating the potential costs of a breach and comparing them to the investment in preventive measures. For example, if we invest $1 million in cybersecurity and prevent a breach that could have cost us $10 million in damages, legal fees, and lost business, that's a significant return. Additionally, we can look at metrics like customer retention, which improves when customers feel their data is secure."

Mike nodded, now more engaged. "So, you're saying we should view cybersecurity as not just a defense mechanism but as a strategic investment that pays off in both risk mitigation and business growth?"

"Right," Nick affirmed. "It's about shifting the perspective from seeing cybersecurity as a necessary expense to viewing it as an enabler of business continuity and growth. With strong cybersecurity, we're not just avoiding costs, we're also positioning ourselves as a reliable and trustworthy partner in the market."

Mike leaned back in his chair, a thoughtful expression on his face. "You've given me a lot to think about, Nick. I appreciate you framing it this way. It makes a lot more sense now."

Nick smiled, feeling a sense of accomplishment. "I'm glad to hear that, Mike. I believe that with the right approach, we can turn our cybersecurity efforts into a real asset for the company."

Meeting with Kevin

Nick met with Kevin, the logistics expert with global experience. Kevin's office was filled with maps and models of various supply chains, showcasing the complexity of his work.

"Kevin, I appreciate you meeting with me," Nick said, shaking Kevin's hand. "I wanted to discuss how our cybersecurity efforts impact our operations and logistics. But first, I'd like to understand what your main concerns are."

Kevin leaned forward, his interest piqued. "Cybersecurity is critical for our operations, Nick. Any disruption can cause significant delays in our supply chain. My main concern is how these cybersecurity measures ensure the continuity and efficiency of our logistics operations."

Nick smiled, glad to see Kevin's engagement. "Our cybersecurity measures are designed to protect our operational systems from attacks that could disrupt our logistics. For instance, ransomware could lock us out of our systems, halting our operations. By implementing strong cybersecurity protocols, we're ensuring that our internal operations remain uninterrupted and efficient. But I also understand that our protection extends beyond just our systems."

Kevin nodded. "That's crucial. Any delay can have a ripple effect across our entire network. But what about our supply chain partners? How do we ensure they are also secure and don't become weak links in the chain?"

Nick appreciated Kevin's insight. "That's an excellent point. Protecting our supply chain is a critical part of our cybersecurity strategy. We recognize that even if our systems are secure, vulnerabilities within our third-party vendors can still pose significant risks. Therefore, we have a comprehensive third-party risk management program in place."

Kevin's eyes lit up with interest. "Tell me more about this program."

Nick continued, "Our third-party risk management program involves conducting thorough cybersecurity assessments of all our vendors and partners. We ensure they meet our security standards before we engage with them. Additionally, we regularly monitor their security practices and conduct audits to ensure ongoing compliance. This helps us mitigate risks from external sources and maintain the integrity of our supply chain."

Kevin leaned in, clearly interested. "How do you handle situations where a vendor might be reluctant to share their security protocols or doesn't meet our standards?"

Nick was prepared for this question. "In those cases, we approach it as a collaborative effort. We work closely with the vendor to help them understand our security requirements and why they're important. Sometimes, it's about education—helping them see the value of strong cybersecurity measures for their own business, not just ours. If a vendor is reluctant to share information, we explain the necessity of transparency for our partnership to continue. If they still don't meet our standards, we might offer support to help them improve their security, but if they're unwilling or unable to comply, we may have to reconsider the partnership."

Kevin nodded, impressed with the proactive approach. "That's a strong stance, and it's good to hear we're not compromising on security, even if it means making tough decisions. It shows we're serious about maintaining the integrity of our operations."

"Absolutely," Nick replied. "Our goal is to ensure that our entire supply chain is resilient against cyber threats. This not only protects us but also strengthens our relationships with our vendors, as they too become more secure."

Kevin leaned back in his chair, a thoughtful expression on his face. "That makes a lot of sense. It's good to know we're taking a proactive approach to managing third-party risks. One weak link could compromise our entire operation."

"Exactly," Nick said. "By addressing these risks proactively, we're not just protecting our systems but also ensuring the continuity and reliability of our supply chain. This way, we can minimize disruptions and maintain efficient operations, even in the face of potential cyber threats."

Kevin smiled, satisfied with the discussion. "Thank you, Nick. This conversation has been very enlightening. I'm glad to know that our cybersecurity efforts are comprehensive and that we're taking steps to secure our entire supply chain."

Nick felt a sense of accomplishment. "I'm glad to hear that, Kevin. It's all about working together to ensure that our operations run smoothly and securely."

Meeting with Dr. Haversham

Nick was a bit apprehensive about his meeting with Dr. Haversham later that day. The doctor was known for their off-topic questions, but Nick was determined to address their concerns effectively. The meeting was scheduled over Zoom, providing a comfortable setting for a thorough discussion.

"Dr. Haversham, thank you for taking the time to meet with me," Nick said as their face appeared on the screen.

"Of course, Nick," Dr. Haversham replied, adjusting their glasses. "I'm interested in understanding how our cybersecurity measures impact patient safety."

Nick took a deep breath, ready to steer the conversation. "While MedTech Parts doesn't directly handle patient care, we play a crucial role in ensuring that healthcare providers have the equipment and parts they need when they need them. Our cybersecurity measures are essential to maintain the integrity and availability of these parts, ensuring that patient care is not disrupted."

Dr. Haversham nodded, but their expression remained inquisitive. "I understand that. But what about the security of the medical devices themselves? Are we responsible for ensuring their safety?"

"MedTech Parts isn't directly responsible for the security of the medical devices," Nick explained. "However, some parts we supply do drive the internal workings of the equipment. While the security of the devices is ultimately up to the manufacturers, we ensure that our parts are reliable and delivered securely to avoid any potential disruptions."

Dr. Haversham leaned forward, their eyes narrowing slightly. "But what if there were a cyber attack that compromised the parts during the manufacturing process? How do we ensure that the components we supply haven't been tampered with?"

Nick appreciated the depth of the question and responded thoughtfully. "We have stringent quality control and security protocols in place during the manufacturing process to prevent tampering. Our facilities are equipped with advanced security measures, including monitoring systems that detect unauthorized access or changes to our manufacturing lines. Additionally, we work closely with our suppliers to ensure that their processes are equally secure. Any anomaly is thoroughly investigated before the parts are approved for distribution."

Dr. Haversham seemed to ponder this for a moment. "I see. But what about the information we handle? How do we protect the sensitive data of our customers and employees?"

Nick was pleased to move the conversation to a topic where he could provide more concrete reassurances. "We take protecting customer and employee information very seriously. Our cybersecurity measures include robust encryption protocols, regular security audits, and continuous monitoring to detect and prevent any unauthorized access to our systems. This ensures that sensitive information is kept safe and secure."

Dr. Haversham's face softened a bit, showing a hint of satisfaction. "That's reassuring, Nick. Data breaches can have severe implications, not just for the company but also for the individuals affected. How do we ensure that our customers are informed and protected in the event of a breach?"

Nick appreciated the thoughtful question. "In the event of a breach, we have a comprehensive incident response plan in place. This includes immediate containment measures, a thorough investigation to understand the scope of the breach, and transparent communication with affected parties. We inform our customers promptly and provide guidance on steps they can take to protect themselves. Our goal is to handle such situations with integrity and transparency, minimizing any potential harm."

Dr. Haversham nodded approvingly. "That sounds thorough, Nick. It's good to know that we have strong measures in place to protect sensitive information. Patient safety might not be directly within our purview, but ensuring that providers have reliable equipment and that their data is secure is certainly a step in the right direction."

Nick felt a sense of relief. "Absolutely, Dr. Haversham. Our commitment to cybersecurity is part of our broader mission to support healthcare providers and ensure they can deliver the best care possible."

Dr. Haversham smiled. "Thank you, Nick. This has been a very enlightening discussion. Keep up the good work."

Nick smiled back, feeling accomplished. "Thank you, Dr. Haversham. Your insights are invaluable, and I'll make sure to keep you updated on our cybersecurity efforts."

Key Takeaways

1. **Individual Concerns**: Address each board member's specific concerns to build trust and understanding.
2. **Framing Communication**: Frame cybersecurity issues in terms that are relevant and relatable to each board member's area of focus.
3. **Building Trust**: Use one-on-one meetings to build trust and ensure that board members feel heard and valued.
4. **Practical Examples**: Provide concrete examples to illustrate the impact of cybersecurity measures on different aspects of the business.

Discussion Prompts

1. How can you tailor your communication to address the specific concerns of different stakeholders in your organization?
2. What strategies can you use to build trust with board members or other senior leaders?
3. How can framing your message in different contexts improve understanding and support for your initiatives?

9

RISK

Nick had made significant progress in understanding how to effectively communicate with the board. He had learned about bridging information asymmetry, managing the affect heuristic, and building trust through reducing self-orientation. But there was one more crucial element he needed to master: communicating risk scoring. Kathy had emphasized the importance of presenting risks in a way that the board could understand and act upon.

Nick arrived at the coffee shop, eager to dive into this complex topic. Kathy greeted him warmly, and they quickly settled into their discussion.

"Good to see you, Nick," Kathy said, smiling as she took a sip of her coffee. "How did your one-on-ones with Mike, Kevin, and Dr. Haversham go?"

Nick smiled, feeling a sense of accomplishment. "They went really well, actually. Mike was primarily concerned with the financial stability and cost implications of our cybersecurity measures. We had a deep conversation about how cybersecurity often seems like a cost center, but I reframed it as a strategic investment. I explained how robust security isn't just about avoiding losses from breaches; it can actually protect our financial assets and even create value for the company by building customer trust and opening new opportunities. For example, we talked about how demonstrating our commitment to cybersecurity could differentiate us in the market, attracting customers who are increasingly concerned about their data privacy and security."

Kathy leaned forward, her interest piqued. "That's a great way to frame it. How did Mike respond to that?"

Nick nodded, recalling the conversation. "He seemed intrigued by the idea that cybersecurity could be a value driver, not just a cost. I could see him starting to think about cybersecurity as part of our competitive advantage. He even mentioned that we should explore

DOI: 10.1201/9781003597407-9

how we can use our strong security posture in our marketing materials to highlight our commitment to protecting customer data."

Kathy smiled approvingly. "Sounds like you really got him thinking beyond just the costs. That's exactly what you want—to shift the board's perspective to see cybersecurity as integral to the business strategy."

"Exactly," Nick agreed. "Then there was my meeting with Kevin. He was very focused on the operational side—specifically, the potential disruptions in our supply chain. He's got a real understanding of how even minor disruptions can cascade into major delays. I assured him that our third-party risk management program is designed to ensure that our vendors meet our security standards, which helps maintain the integrity of our supply chain. But we didn't stop there. Kevin raised concerns about the complexities of coordinating with multiple vendors, especially on a global scale. We discussed how our cybersecurity measures include regular audits and assessments of our vendors, ensuring they are consistently up to par."

Kathy nodded approvingly. "Kevin's concerns are very valid. Supply chain security is critical, and it sounds like you gave him the reassurance he needed. How did he react to the idea of regular vendor assessments?"

Nick smiled. "He was actually quite relieved to hear that we're taking such a proactive approach. He mentioned that he had been worried about the weakest link in the chain, so to speak, and was glad to know we have measures in place to mitigate those risks. We even talked about the possibility of bringing in some of our key vendors for joint security training, to ensure they fully understand the importance of these protocols [13]."

"That's a fantastic idea," Kathy said, impressed. "By involving the vendors directly, you're not only securing your own operations but also building stronger relationships with your partners."

Nick continued. "And then there was my meeting with Dr. Haversham. As you might expect, they were focused on patient safety. He asked some challenging questions about the potential impact of cybersecurity failures on the medical devices that use our parts. I explained that while MedTech Parts isn't directly responsible for the security of the devices themselves, we play a crucial role in ensuring the reliability and secure delivery of our parts. We talked about how a breach in our supply chain could delay the delivery of critical components, potentially impacting patient care. I also emphasized our commitment to protecting customer and employee information, and how our encryption protocols and regular audits help safeguard that data. It seemed to reassure them, especially when I connected it back to the broader implications for patient trust and safety."

Kathy smiled, clearly impressed. "It sounds like you really understood what each of them needed to hear. By addressing their specific concerns and framing cybersecurity in a way that relates directly to their priorities, you're making it clear that you're not just thinking about security in isolation—you're thinking about how it supports the entire business."

Nick felt a renewed sense of confidence as he reflected on his recent conversations. "It's all about showing them that cybersecurity isn't just my concern—it's everyone's concern, and it impacts every part of the business. And by tailoring my communication to address what each of them cares about most, I'm able to make a stronger case for the importance of our cybersecurity initiatives."

"Exactly," Kathy agreed. "Framing is key. Now, let's dive into our discussion on risk."

"Kathy, I've actually been thinking a lot about risk scoring," Nick began. "It's such a critical part of our cybersecurity strategy, but it's also one of the most challenging to explain to the board. Can you help me understand how to communicate it effectively?"

Kathy nodded. "Absolutely, Nick. Risk scoring is a complex but essential part of cybersecurity. It's about evaluating and prioritizing risks to ensure that the most critical issues are addressed first. The challenge is making these evaluations understandable to non-technical stakeholders. Let's start by discussing the basics of risk scoring."

Nick took out his notebook, ready to absorb as much information as possible.

"Risk scoring involves quantifying the potential impact and likelihood of various cybersecurity threats," Kathy explained. "This can be done using quantitative methods, qualitative methods, or a combination of both. Quantitative methods rely on numerical data to create models, while qualitative methods use expert judgment to assess risks [11]."

Nick nodded, jotting down notes. "I understand that part. But I've read that data for building quantitative models in cybersecurity is often lacking, and the industry is constantly changing."

"That's correct," Kathy said. "The half-life of cybersecurity data is short due to the rapidly evolving threat landscape [21]. This makes it difficult to rely solely on quantitative models. For instance, while methods like FAIR, Nexpose, and the approaches outlined by Hubbard and Seiersen provide structured frameworks, they often depend on broad estimates [19]. On the other hand, risk matrices and purely qualitative methods can sometimes be as unreliable as random guessing [7]."

Nick frowned. "So, what's the solution? How do we effectively score and communicate these risks?"

Kathy smiled. "A combined approach often works best. Use quantitative data where it's available and supplement it with qualitative assessments to fill in the gaps [6]. Let's break down some steps to help you communicate risk scoring effectively to the board:

1. **Explain the Basics**: Start with a simple explanation of what risk scoring is and why it's important. Use analogies if necessary. For example, compare it to credit scoring, where various factors are evaluated to determine a person's creditworthiness.
2. **Use Clear Metrics**: Clearly define the metrics you use to score risks. This could include factors like likelihood, impact, and vulnerability. Make sure these metrics are understandable to non-technical stakeholders.
3. **Present Both Qualitative and Quantitative Data**: Show how you use both types of data to create a comprehensive risk score. Explain that while quantitative data provides a solid foundation, qualitative insights from experts help fill in the gaps.
4. **Visual Aids**: Use charts, graphs, and other visual tools to make the information more digestible. Visual aids can simplify complex data and highlight key points.
5. **Prioritize Risks**: Clearly show how the risk scores help prioritize which threats need immediate attention and resources. Explain the reasoning behind the prioritization.

6. **Highlight Preventive Measures**: Pair the risk scores with the preventive measures you're taking to mitigate these risks. This helps the board understand not just the threats but also the proactive steps being taken to address them.

7. **Provide Context**: Always provide context for the risk scores. For instance, explain how a high-risk score for a particular vulnerability impacts the business operations, finances, or reputation.

8. **Use the CRISM Tool**: If you feel comfortable, use the Cyber Risk Scoring and Mitigation (CRISM) tool and understand how it helps prioritize risks [21]. Use its components, such as automatic discovery of vulnerabilities, lateral propagation analysis, security metrics, prioritized mitigation plans, and compliance with cybersecurity frameworks."

Nick scribbled furiously, trying to capture every detail. "This makes a lot of sense. Can you give me an example of how you've communicated risk scoring to a board in the past?"

"Sure," Kathy said. "In one instance, I had to explain the risks associated with a potential data breach. I started by explaining the concept of risk scoring using the analogy of a credit score. I then presented the risks in a manner that resonated with the board members based on their roles and concerns [4]. For the CFO, I emphasized the potential financial impacts and how our preventive measures would protect the company's bottom line. For the COO, I highlighted how these measures would ensure operational continuity and avoid disruptions."

Nick looked impressed. "That sounds incredibly effective. By combining quantitative and qualitative data, using visual aids, and providing context, you made the information both accessible and actionable."

"Exactly," Kathy said. "The goal is to make the board feel informed and confident in their decision-making. When they understand the risks and the measures being taken to mitigate them, they can better allocate resources and support your initiatives."

Nick then recalled the importance of answering the "What's in it for me?" question for the board members. He shared his thoughts with Kathy. "I understand that each board member needs to see how the risks and mitigations directly impact their areas of concern. This means using the right balance of quantitative and qualitative data based on what they value most."

"Absolutely," Kathy agreed. "It's crucial to meet them where they are. Data shows that executive risk perception of technical and aggregated risks is similar. If they want quantitative data, provide that. If they prefer qualitative assessments, use those. For example, I once had an executive who wanted a heat map with bubbles. The heat map showed the likelihood and impact, and the size of the bubble represented the level of control we had over each risk. While not statistically the most accurate tool, it was an effective way to present the information visually in the way they wanted it."

Nick nodded, appreciating the practical advice. "It makes sense to provide information in a manner the decision maker wants. I could incorporate other tools as well, such as loss exceedance curves and their preferred visuals."

Kathy smiled. "You're on the right track, Nick. Keep focusing on clarity and relevance. You've got this."

As their meeting wrapped up, Nick felt a renewed sense of purpose. He knew that by effectively communicating risk scoring, he could further strengthen the board's confidence in his leadership and improve the organization's cybersecurity posture.

Back at the office, Nick began preparing for the next board meeting with renewed enthusiasm. He started creating visual aids, tailoring his explanations to each board member's concerns, and ensuring that his risk scores and metrics were clear and actionable. He also took some time to reflect on Kathy's advice about meeting board members where they are. He realized that understanding the preferred communication style of each board member was just as important as the content of the communication itself.

Nick decided to create a few different versions of his risk scoring report. One would focus more heavily on quantitative data, with detailed charts and numerical analyses, for board members like Mike, who appreciated a data-driven approach. Another version would be more qualitative, using scenarios and narratives to explain the risks and their potential impacts, tailored for members like Dr. Haversham, who preferred to understand the broader implications rather than getting lost in the numbers.

He also started working on his presentation skills, practicing how to explain complex concepts in simple, relatable terms. He knew that no matter how well he understood the risks, it wouldn't matter if he couldn't communicate them effectively. He wanted to ensure that when he spoke to the board, he could do so with clarity and confidence, making the risks and the importance of mitigation efforts crystal clear.

Nick was confident that these efforts would pay off. By preparing thoroughly and considering each board member's perspective, he was on his way to becoming a more effective communicator and a trusted advisor to the board. The journey was still ahead of him, but he felt more prepared to face the challenges that lay ahead.

Key Takeaways

1. **Use Clear Metrics**: Define the metrics used to score risks in an understandable way.
2. **Combine Data**: Use both quantitative and qualitative data to create comprehensive risk scores.
3. **Visual Aids**: Utilize charts, graphs, and other visual tools to present risk scores clearly.
4. **Relevant Framing**: Tailor the presentation of risks to resonate with different stakeholders' priorities.
5. **Prioritize Risks**: Show how risk scores help prioritize threats and allocate resources.
6. **Highlight Preventive Measures**: Pair risk scores with preventive actions to provide a complete picture.
7. **Provide Context**: Explain the impact of risks in a business context to make them relatable and actionable.
8. **Answering "What's in it for me?"**: Always ensure that the board understands how the risks and mitigations impact their specific concerns.

Discussion Prompts

1. How can you effectively communicate risk scores to non-technical stakeholders?

2. What visual aids can you use to make complex risk information more digestible?
3. How can you combine quantitative and qualitative data to create a comprehensive risk assessment?

10

BOARD PREPARATIONS

Nick had come a long way since his initial struggles with the board. With Kathy's guidance, he had learned about bridging information asymmetry, managing the affect heuristic, building trust, and understanding his audience. Now, it was time to put all of these lessons into practice as he prepared for the upcoming board meeting.

Nick began by reviewing his notes from his meetings with Kathy. He made sure that his presentation would highlight the positive impacts of cybersecurity on business goals, financial health, and operational efficiency. He also focused on framing his message to address the board members' specific concerns and priorities.

Nick knew that one-on-one meetings with key board members would be crucial for building trust and understanding their concerns. He scheduled meetings with Kevin, Mike, and Sharon, the COO, to preview his presentation and gather their feedback.

Kevin, a logistics expert with broad global experience, was primarily concerned with operational disruptions. From his conversation with Kevin, Nick learned that Kevin wanted concrete examples of how cybersecurity measures would ensure operational continuity and minimize downtime. Kevin's concerns were directly tied to the supply chain and the impact of third-party risks. Nick planned to highlight how MedTech Parts' third-party risk management program ensured vendors met security standards, thereby maintaining the integrity of their supply chain.

Mike, a board member with a CFO background, was focused on the financial implications of cybersecurity. During their one-on-one, Mike had asked for specific numbers and a clear cost-benefit analysis. Nick prepared a detailed section in his presentation showing how investments in cybersecurity measures could lead to significant cost savings by preventing data breaches, avoiding fines, and maintaining customer trust. He also planned to link these savings to the company's

DOI: 10.1201/9781003597407-10

quarterly financial targets, making the benefits more tangible for the board.

Dr. Haversham, who was focused on patient safety, posed a unique challenge. Although MedTech Parts didn't directly impact patient care, their products were essential for the reliability of medical equipment. Nick planned to emphasize the company's commitment to ensuring the secure delivery of parts and protecting customer and employee information. He knew that addressing Dr. Haversham's concerns would require framing the conversation around the broader implications of cybersecurity on the company's reputation and trustworthiness.

With these insights in mind, Nick also decided to meet with his team to get a sense of the day-to-day operations and gather examples of how their cybersecurity efforts were making a difference. He wanted to ensure his presentation was grounded in real-world examples and could demonstrate the tangible benefits of their initiatives.

In the operations center, Nick gathered his team for a brief meeting. The room buzzed with the hum of computers and the quiet intensity of analysts focused on their monitors. Nick could see the dedication on their faces and knew that their insights would be invaluable for his upcoming presentation.

"I need your input on how our cybersecurity measures have made a real difference in our operations," Nick began, looking around at his team. "Can you share some recent examples of incidents we've prevented or disruptions we've minimized?"

Jane, one of the lead analysts, immediately raised her hand. "Just last month, we detected and neutralized a phishing attempt that could have compromised our entire email system. It was a sophisticated attack, designed to bypass our initial defenses by mimicking internal communications. Our proactive monitoring flagged it almost immediately. Within minutes, we were able to isolate the affected accounts and block the malicious emails before they spread any further. Because of our quick response, there was no data loss, no downtime, and we avoided what could have been a significant breach."

Nick nodded, impressed by the quick thinking and efficiency of the team. "Great example, Jane. That's exactly the kind of real-world impact the board needs to hear about. Not just that we're preventing breaches, but that we're doing so with minimal disruption to our operations. It shows the value of our ongoing vigilance."

He looked around the room, his eyes landing on Tom, another senior analyst. "What about our third-party vendors? Have we had any issues there that could have impacted our operations?"

Tom leaned forward, tapping a few keys on his laptop to bring up some notes. "We've had a few vendors fail to meet our security standards initially, but our rigorous assessment process and continuous monitoring have ensured they quickly brought their practices up to par. For instance, one of our key suppliers for critical components had outdated security protocols that could have exposed us to significant risks. We flagged this during our initial review and worked closely with them to implement the necessary upgrades. Within two weeks, they were fully compliant with our standards, and we've been monitoring them closely ever since."

Nick could see the importance of this example. "Tom, that's excellent. It highlights not just our internal security measures but also how we're actively managing external risks. The board needs to understand that our supply chain security is just as critical as our internal defenses."

"Absolutely," Tom agreed. "And just to add, during that process, we also discovered that another vendor, who was providing us with some non-critical services, had been storing our data in a way that didn't meet our encryption standards. We identified the issue through our continuous monitoring, and when we brought it to their attention, they weren't able to address it quickly enough. So, we decided to terminate the contract and move to a more secure provider. This decision not only protected our data but also sent a strong message to all our vendors that we take security seriously."

Nick appreciated the proactive approach the team had taken. "That's a powerful example, Tom. It shows that we're not just passively relying on our vendors to meet our standards—we're actively holding them accountable and making tough decisions when they don't. It's about protecting our operations from every angle."

He turned his attention to the rest of the team. "What else? Any other incidents or preventive measures that have made a significant impact?"

Sarah, who had been quietly listening, spoke up next. "We've been seeing an increase in DDoS attacks aimed at our customer-facing platforms. Last quarter, we implemented a new AI-driven defense system that can detect and mitigate these attacks in real-time. We've already seen it in action twice in the last month. Both times, the system neutralized the attacks within seconds, and there was zero impact on our customers. They never even knew anything was happening."

Nick was pleased to hear this. "That's fantastic, Sarah. Not only does it show the effectiveness of our new technology, but it also demonstrates our commitment to maintaining service continuity for our customers. This kind of seamless protection is exactly what the board will want to hear about."

"Exactly," Sarah continued. "And just to add, we've also been using the data from these incidents to improve our threat models. Every time we neutralize an attack, we feed that information back into our system, so it's constantly learning and getting better at defending against future threats."

Nick made a note of this, recognizing the importance of continuous improvement. "That's an important point, Sarah. It shows that we're not just reacting to threats—we're evolving with them, making our defenses stronger with each incident."

He looked around the room one last time, making sure everyone had the opportunity to contribute. "Anyone else? Even small incidents or changes can make a big difference."

Raj, one of the newer members of the team, hesitated before speaking up. "Well, it might seem minor, but we've been doing some work on insider threat detection. We recently implemented a new system that monitors for unusual activity within our internal networks. A few weeks ago, it flagged an employee who was accessing files they normally wouldn't. It turned out they weren't doing anything malicious—just looking up some old project data—but the system allowed us to catch it early and have a conversation with them before it could become an issue."

Nick smiled, appreciating Raj's input. "That's not minor at all, Raj. Insider threats can be just as dangerous as external ones, and it's crucial that we have systems in place to detect and address them early. The board needs to know that we're protecting the company from all angles—inside and out."

He took a moment to look around at his team, feeling a deep sense of pride. "You've all done incredible work. The examples you've shared today are exactly what I need to make our case to the board. They show that our cybersecurity efforts aren't just about preventing hypothetical threats—they're about making real, tangible differences in our day-to-day operations. Thank you for your input and for all the hard work you put in every day to keep us safe."

The team exchanged satisfied smiles, knowing that their efforts were not only being recognized but also making a significant impact on the company's overall security posture.

With his team's insights and examples in hand, Nick felt more pre-pared than ever for his upcoming presentation. He knew that these concrete examples would resonate with the board and help them see the true value of the company's cybersecurity initiatives.

Nick nodded, appreciating the team's input. "These examples are perfect. They show the board that our cybersecurity measures are not just theoretical but have real, positive impacts on our operations."

Armed with these real-world examples and the insights from his one-on-one meetings, Nick felt more confident about his upcoming presentation. Now he needed to meet with Sharon.

Sharon, the COO, was focused on maintaining business continuity and ensuring that operations ran smoothly. Nick framed his message to show how cybersecurity measures would protect the company's operations and ensure continuity.

"Sharon, our cybersecurity initiatives are designed to keep our operations running smoothly and avoid any disruptions," Nick began. "By implementing these measures, we can protect our systems from potential threats and ensure that our business continues to operate efficiently."

Sharon appreciated Nick's focus on operational impacts. "I like where you're going with this, Nick. Can you provide some examples of how these measures have protected our operations in the past?"

Nick shared success stories of how MedTech Parts had prevented operational disruptions through proactive cybersecurity measures. He also explained how ongoing monitoring and updates ensure continued protection.

Sharon then suggested they do a dry run of the presentation. Nick welcomed the opportunity, knowing Sharon's experience with presenting to the board would be invaluable. He set up his slides and began his presentation, highlighting the key points he had refined.

Sharon listened intently, occasionally nodding as Nick went through his slides. As Nick finished, she leaned forward, her expression thoughtful but encouraging. "Nick, that was a solid presentation. You've clearly put a lot of thought into addressing the board's concerns. However, I have a few suggestions that might help you fine-tune your approach."

Nick, bracing himself for feedback, leaned in, ready to absorb every word. He knew that Sharon's insights could be the key to refining his presentation.

"First," Sharon began, "when you talk about the financial impacts of our cybersecurity investments, make sure you tie those impacts directly to our current financial goals. The board is going to want to see how these investments align with our broader business strategy, particularly in terms of cost savings and return on investment. Use specific numbers and projections that the board is already familiar with. For example, if our quarterly financial target includes reducing operational costs by a certain percentage, show how our cybersecurity measures contribute to that goal. Connect the dots between your initiatives and the financial outcomes the board is focused on."

Nick nodded, jotting down notes. "So, rather than just talking about the potential cost savings from avoiding breaches, I should quantify those savings in terms of their impact on our quarterly financial targets. For instance, if we've estimated that a potential breach could cost us $5 million in fines and lost revenue, I could tie that to our goal of reducing costs by 10% this quarter."

"Exactly," Sharon said, a satisfied smile forming. "When you can translate the impact of cybersecurity into the financial language the board understands, it becomes much easier for them to see the value in what you're proposing. And don't forget to highlight any past successes—like how preventing a specific breach saved us a significant amount of money last quarter. Real examples make the abstract numbers more concrete."

Nick could see how this approach would resonate with the board. "I'll make sure to include those real examples and clearly show how they've contributed to our financial goals."

"Good," Sharon continued. "Next, when you discuss operational continuity, you need to get a bit more granular. The board needs to see the direct correlation between our cybersecurity measures and the ability to maintain critical business operations. I'd suggest including a brief overview of our most critical operations—such as our supply chain logistics, customer service platforms, and manufacturing processes—and then demonstrate how our cybersecurity measures protect each one."

Nick scribbled down more notes, thinking back to his one-on-one meetings. "So, for Kevin, for example, I could talk about how our third-party risk management program protects the integrity of our supply chain, preventing disruptions that could delay product delivery. And for Mike, I might focus on how protecting our customer service platforms ensures we maintain high levels of customer satisfaction, which directly impacts revenue."

"Precisely," Sharon agreed, her tone affirming Nick's thought process.

"You need to show them that cybersecurity isn't just an IT concern—it's a business continuity concern. And that means breaking it down operation by operation. If they can see that each critical part of our business is protected, they'll be much more likely to support further investments in cybersecurity. Also, consider bringing up specific scenarios where our cybersecurity measures have prevented operational disruptions. Remember the issue Tom mentioned about the vendor not meeting our security standards? That's a perfect example of how we proactively protected our supply chain from potential vulnerabilities."

Nick nodded thoughtfully. "I'll expand that section to include these specific operations and tie them directly to our cybersecurity measures. I'll also make sure to emphasize the operational continuity aspect, using real examples to illustrate the point."

"Lastly," Sharon said, her tone becoming more advisory, "you need to be prepared for the questions that might come up. The board will appreciate clear, concise answers. If you're unsure about something, it's okay to say you'll follow up with more details later, but try to anticipate their main concerns and have answers ready. You've learned a lot from your meetings with Kathy and the other board members—use that knowledge to predict the kinds of questions they might ask."

Nick thought for a moment, reflecting on the concerns each board member had expressed during their one-on-ones. "So, Mike might ask about the long-term financial implications of our cybersecurity investments, while Kevin could be concerned about the impact of new security measures on our supply chain efficiency. And Dr. Haversham might have questions about how our cybersecurity initiatives indirectly support patient safety. I should prepare specific responses for each of these areas."

Sharon smiled, clearly pleased with Nick's proactive approach.

"Exactly. And remember, if a question catches you off guard, it's better to acknowledge that you don't have the answer right now but will get back to them with the information. It shows transparency and builds trust. Take the look-up—when you don't know something, admit it, and let them know you'll follow up. This way, you avoid any potential missteps and show that you're committed to providing accurate, thorough information."

Nick felt a sense of relief mixed with determination. Sharon's feedback had given him a clear path to refine his presentation and approach. "Thank you, Sharon. This is exactly what I needed to take my presentation to the next level. I'll make those adjustments and practice my responses so I'm fully prepared."

"You're doing great, Nick," Sharon said encouragingly. "Just remember, the key is to connect with the board on their terms—speak their language, address their concerns, and always be ready to back up your points with solid data and examples. You've got this."

With Sharon's detailed feedback and his growing confidence, Nick was ready to make the final adjustments to his presentation. He knew that with the right preparation, he could communicate the importance of cybersecurity in a way that would resonate with the board and secure their support for the initiatives he was championing.

Key Takeaways

1. **Prepare Thoroughly**: Apply learned strategies and gather feedback from key stakeholders.
2. **Engage in One-on-One Meetings**: Tailor your message to address specific concerns and priorities.

3. **Practice and Rehearse**: Ensure clear, concise communication and effective framing.
4. **Seek Feedback**: Use feedback from experienced colleagues to refine your approach.
5. **Build Confidence**: Provide clear answers and highlight positive impacts to build trust.

Discussion Prompts

1. How can you prepare effectively for a board meeting to address cybersecurity concerns?
2. What strategies can you use to engage and build trust with board members during a presentation?
3. How can you ensure that your communication is clear, relevant, and actionable for your audience?

11

THE NEXT BOARD MEETING

The day of the board meeting had arrived. Nick felt a mix of nervousness and excitement as he prepared to present his updated cybersecurity strategy to the board. He knew that this was his chance to show how much he had learned and to build trust with the board members.

As Nick stood in his office, he took a moment to review his preparation. He had spent countless hours refining his presentation, rehearsing his delivery, and anticipating potential questions. The one-on-one meetings with board members had been invaluable, offering him deep insights into their concerns and priorities. He knew that today's meeting was not just about delivering a presentation but about solidifying his role as a strategic leader within the company. Nick had also taken the time to connect with his team that morning, gathering any last-minute updates and reassurances. The calm focus of his team gave him an added boost of confidence. They were ready, and so was he.

As Nick entered the boardroom, he glanced around and saw familiar faces. Kevin, Mike, Dr. Haversham, Sharon, and the other board members were already seated, engaged in quiet conversations. Nick took a deep breath and began setting up his presentation.

"Good morning, everyone," Nick started, once everyone was settled. "Thank you for giving me the opportunity to present our updated cybersecurity strategy. Today, I want to focus on how our initiatives support our business goals, ensure operational continuity, and protect our financial health."

Nick launched into his presentation, starting with an overview of the key points. He highlighted the positive impacts of cybersecurity on business goals, financial health, and operational efficiency. He made sure to frame his message to address the specific concerns and priorities of each board member, just as he had practiced.

As he progressed through his slides, Nick made sure to integrate the real-world examples his team had shared with him. When

DOI: 10.1201/9781003597407-11

discussing the impact of phishing attacks, he detailed how their proactive monitoring had neutralized a potentially catastrophic breach just last month.

"Our advanced threat detection systems detected an anomaly that could have compromised our email infrastructure, potentially leading to significant operational downtime. However, because of our rapid response, the threat was contained within minutes, and there was no interruption to our services. As we continue to enhance our cybersecurity measures," Nick continued, "we're not just protecting our systems but also supporting our business objectives. Our initiatives are designed to ensure operational continuity, protect our financial health, and maintain our reputation in the industry."

Kevin leaned forward, nodding along as Nick spoke about the operational benefits of cybersecurity. "Nick, can you explain more about the specific measures in place to prevent operational disruptions?" Kevin asked.

"Certainly, Kevin," Nick replied confidently. "We've implemented advanced threat detection systems that continuously monitor for unusual activity. These systems allow us to respond swiftly, minimizing any operational impact. For instance, last month, our system detected an anomaly that could have led to significant downtime, but we addressed it within minutes, ensuring seamless operations. Additionally, our third-party risk management program ensures that all our vendors meet stringent security standards, so there's no weak link in our supply chain."

Nick paused for a moment, allowing the information to sink in before continuing. "Beyond our immediate internal measures, we've also instituted a more rigorous assessment process for our supply chain partners. For example, we recently identified a vendor who initially failed to meet our security benchmarks. By working closely with them, we were able to elevate their security posture to align with our standards. This proactive approach not only prevents disruptions but also reinforces our overall operational resilience."

Mike, who had been listening intently, raised a hand. "Nick, I appreciate the operational focus, but can you provide further details on the cost-benefit analysis of these cybersecurity investments? How do these measures impact our financial health?"

Nick smiled, ready for this question. "Absolutely, Mike. By investing in these cybersecurity measures, we're not just preventing breaches but also avoiding the high costs associated with them, such as fines, legal fees, and lost revenue. For example, a recent study showed that companies with robust cybersecurity programs experience 40% fewer breaches, translating to significant cost savings. Our proactive approach protects our bottom line and ensures a positive return on investment."

Nick continued, "Let me give you a concrete example. Last quarter, we avoided a potential breach that could have resulted in a loss of approximately $2 million in fines and lost business. By investing $500,000 in our cybersecurity infrastructure, we not only avoided that loss but also protected our brand's reputation, which is invaluable. Additionally, these investments directly contribute to our quarterly financial goals by safeguarding revenue streams and reducing potential liabilities."

Mike seemed satisfied with the explanation, but Nick pressed on, wanting to ensure his message was fully understood. "Moreover, the cost savings from preventing a major breach allow us to allocate more resources to strategic initiatives like expanding into new markets or accelerating product development. In this way, cybersecurity is not just a defensive measure but a strategic enabler of growth."

Dr. Haversham, who had been quiet until now, spoke up. "Nick, while the financial and operational aspects are important, how do these measures impact patient safety? MedTech Parts provides critical components for medical equipment. How does our cybersecurity strategy ensure that these parts are safe and reliable?"

Nick acknowledged Dr. Haversham's concern with a nod. "Dr. Haversham, while MedTech Parts doesn't directly handle patient care, we play a crucial role in ensuring that healthcare providers have reliable and secure equipment. Our cybersecurity measures ensure the integrity and availability of our parts. For example, we secure our supply chain to prevent counterfeit or compromised components from entering the market. Additionally, we protect sensitive customer and employee information to maintain trust and compliance with industry standards."

Nick took a breath, preparing to address the deeper implications. "It's important to understand that any disruption in the supply chain, especially for medical components, could have downstream effects on patient safety. By ensuring that our parts are not only reliable but also securely delivered, we are indirectly supporting the safety and well-being of patients. Our security protocols ensure that no compromised parts ever make it to the healthcare providers, thus maintaining the highest standards of quality and safety. Additionally, we conduct regular audits and compliance checks, particularly for components that are critical in medical devices, to ensure that they meet all necessary regulatory standards."

Sharon, with her extensive experience, asked for clarification on how these measures aligned with the company's strategic goals. "Nick, can you elaborate on how our cybersecurity initiatives align with our broader strategic objectives?"

"Certainly, Sharon," Nick replied. "Our cybersecurity strategy is directly aligned with our business goals. For example, by ensuring operational continuity, we're able to meet our production and delivery targets, which supports our growth objectives. Financially, by preventing costly breaches, we're able to allocate more resources toward innovation and market expansion. And by protecting our reputation, we maintain the trust of our customers and partners, which is crucial for long-term success."

Sharon leaned forward, her interest clearly piqued. "Can you give us more specifics on how these cybersecurity measures tie into our plans for market expansion? How do they support our goal of becoming a leader in the industry?"

Nick was ready for this. "Absolutely, Sharon. As we expand into new markets, particularly in regions with stringent data protection laws, our robust cybersecurity posture becomes a competitive advantage. We're already seeing this play out in Europe, where our commitment to GDPR compliance has opened doors to new partnerships. By demonstrating that we can securely handle customer data and protect intellectual property, we're not only complying with local regulations but also positioning ourselves as a trusted partner in these new markets. This trust translates into stronger relationships with distributors, more favorable terms with suppliers, and increased customer loyalty—all of which are crucial for our market expansion strategy."

The CEO, who had been listening intently, smiled and addressed the room. "Nick, thank you for this comprehensive and clear presentation. It's evident that our cybersecurity strategy is in capable hands. Your efforts not only protect our company but also support our overall business objectives. Please continue to keep us updated as you manage our cybersecurity efforts."

Nick felt a wave of relief and accomplishment as the meeting concluded. He managed to convey the importance of cybersecurity in a way that resonated with each board member's concerns, effectively connecting technical details to business outcomes. He knew this was just the beginning—continuing to build and maintain this trust would require ongoing effort and clear communication. But for now, he could take pride knowing that he had successfully bridged the gap between cybersecurity and the broader business strategy.

As he walked back to his office, Nick reflected on the journey so far. He realized that the key to effective communication was not just about presenting data but making it relevant and understandable for his audience. By closing the information asymmetry gap, managing the affect heuristic, building trust, and understanding his audience, he had made significant strides in his role as a CISO.

Nick paused outside his office door, taking a moment to savor the feeling of accomplishment. He had come a long way from the nervous, uncertain CISO who struggled to connect with the board. Now, he was a leader who could confidently articulate how cybersecurity supported the company's strategic goals, protected its financial health, and ensured operational continuity. And more importantly, he had earned the trust of the board members, not just as a technical expert, but as a strategic partner.

As he stepped into his office, Nick smiled to himself, feeling a renewed sense of purpose. He knew that with continued effort and support, he could bridge the gap between technical details and business priorities, guiding MedTech Parts towards a more secure future. The challenges ahead were significant, but Nick was ready to face them head-on, confident in his ability to lead and protect the company he had come to care for deeply.

Key Takeaways

1. **Focus on Business Goals**: Highlight how cybersecurity initiatives support overall business objectives.

2. **Tailor Your Message:** Address the specific concerns and priorities of each board member.
3. **Provide Clear Examples:** Use concrete examples to illustrate the benefits of cybersecurity measures.
4. **Confidently Address Questions:** Be prepared to answer questions with clear and detailed explanations.
5. **Reflect and Improve:** Continuously refine your approach based on feedback and experiences.

Discussion Prompts

1. How can you highlight the connection between cybersecurity and overall business goals in your presentations?
2. What strategies can you use to ensure your message resonates with different stakeholders?
3. How can you prepare to confidently address questions and concerns during a board meeting?

12

WRAP-UP

Nick stood at his office window, looking out at the bustling activity below. He felt a deep sense of accomplishment after the successful board meeting. The journey had been challenging, but the growth and insights he had gained were invaluable. Reflecting on his experiences, he knew it was time to consolidate the lessons learned and plan for the future.

Building on Foundations

Nick's journey began with understanding the importance of effective communication. His first board meeting was a wake-up call, revealing the gap between his technical expertise and the board's need for clear, business-focused information. With Kathy's guidance, he learned to bridge this gap by addressing information asymmetry, managing the affect heuristic, building trust, and understanding his audience.

1. **Bridging the Information Asymmetry Gap:**
   - Nick learned to translate complex technical details into business-relevant terms, making cybersecurity understandable and actionable for the board.
   - He emphasized the importance of proactive communication, ensuring the board was always informed about potential risks and the measures taken to mitigate them.

In his initial attempts, Nick had focused heavily on the technical details, assuming the board would appreciate the depth of his expertise. However, as Kathy pointed out, the board needed a broader perspective—one that connected the dots between cybersecurity and business outcomes. Nick realized that while his technical skills were critical, they needed to be framed in a way that aligned with the board's strategic priorities. He began to prioritize clarity over complexity, ensuring that his communication bridged the information asymmetry that had initially hindered his effectiveness.

2. Managing the Affect Heuristic:

- Nick recognized that emotions often influenced the board's decisions. By framing cybersecurity issues in a way that reduced fear and promoted rational thinking, he helped the board make more informed decisions.
- He used relatable analogies and focused on positive outcomes, demonstrating how cybersecurity efforts contributed to the company's overall success.

Nick recalled how Kathy had explained the affect heuristic and its impact on decision-making. He realized that the board's initial reactions were often driven by fear of the unknown—fear that could cloud judgment and lead to hasty decisions. By framing cybersecurity challenges in terms of familiar concepts, like home security or financial audits, Nick was able to shift the board's focus from fear to proactive risk management. This approach not only eased the board's concerns but also allowed them to engage more constructively with the issues at hand.

3. Building Trust by Reducing Self-Orientation:

- Nick understood that trust is built on credibility, reliability, intimacy, and reduced self-orientation. By focusing on the board's needs rather than showcasing his achievements, he built stronger relationships.
- He actively listened to the board members, engaged in one-on-one conversations, and addressed their specific concerns, showing that he valued their input and perspectives.

Nick had initially approached his role with the mindset of proving himself—a natural inclination for someone stepping into a new and challenging position. However, Kathy's advice about reducing self-orientation shifted his focus from showcasing his capabilities to addressing the board's concerns. During his one-on-one meetings,

Nick practiced active listening, ensuring that he truly understood what each board member needed from him. This shift in approach not only built trust but also created a sense of partnership between Nick and the board, making them feel that their input was valued and directly influencing the cybersecurity strategy.

4. **Understanding His Audience:**

- Nick tailored his communication to the specific concerns and priorities of each board member, making his messages more relevant and impactful by answering the question, 'What's in it for me?'
- He engaged in continuous dialogue with the board, ensuring that his strategies aligned with their evolving needs and expectations.

Nick reflected on the diverse concerns of the board members—Kevin's focus on operational continuity, Mike's interest in financial stability, and Dr. Haversham's concerns about patient safety. By tailoring his communication to address these specific concerns, Nick was able to make cybersecurity relevant to each board member's domain. He learned that understanding his audience wasn't just about knowing their roles, but about anticipating their concerns and addressing them directly. This approach transformed his interactions with the board from one-sided presentations into meaningful dialogues.

Enhancing Risk Communication

Risk communication was another critical area where Nick made significant strides. He learned to present risk scoring in a way that was clear and understandable to non-technical stakeholders.

1. **Using Clear Metrics and Visual Aids:**

- Nick defined the metrics used to score risks, ensuring they were understandable to the board.
- He used charts, graphs, and other visual tools to simplify complex data and highlight key points, making the information more digestible.

Nick had initially struggled with how to present risk metrics in a way that was both comprehensive and comprehensible. With Kathy's guidance, he began to experiment with different visual aids—heat maps, graphs, and risk matrices—that could convey the severity and likelihood of risks at a glance. These visual tools, which are just that, tools, proved to be a game-changer in his board presentations, making abstract concepts more tangible and allowing board members to quickly grasp the significance of the data being presented.

2. Combining Quantitative and Qualitative Data:

- Nick combined quantitative data with qualitative assessments, providing a comprehensive risk score that the board could trust.
- He emphasized the importance of context, explaining how high-risk scores impacted business operations, finances, and reputation.

Recognizing the limitations of purely quantitative data in the ever-changing cybersecurity landscape, Nick adopted a hybrid approach. By supplementing hard data with qualitative insights from his team and industry experts, he was able to provide a more nuanced view of the risks facing the company. This balanced approach allowed him to convey not only the severity of potential threats but also the rationale behind the company's prioritization of certain risks over others, which in turn strengthened the board's confidence in his leadership.

3. Highlighting Preventive Measures:

- Nick paired risk scores with the preventive measures taken to mitigate these risks, demonstrating the proactive steps being taken to protect the company.
- He provided concrete examples of incidents prevented and disruptions minimized, showing the tangible benefits of their cybersecurity efforts.

Nick realized that it wasn't enough to simply present risks—he needed to show the board how those risks were being actively managed and mitigated. By highlighting specific examples of incidents his team had prevented, such as the phishing attack that was neutralized before it could cause harm, Nick was able to demonstrate the effectiveness of their cybersecurity efforts. This not only reassured the board but also underscored the value of continued investment in cybersecurity.

Future Steps

As Nick looked to the future, he knew that continuous improvement and adaptation were key to maintaining and enhancing the board's trust and confidence in his leadership.

1. Continuous Learning and Adaptation:

- Nick committed to staying updated with the latest trends and best practices in cybersecurity, ensuring that his strategies remained relevant and effective.
- He planned to engage in ongoing professional development, attending conferences and networking with other CISOs to share insights and learn from their experiences.

Nick's journey had taught him the importance of continuous learning—not just for himself, but for his entire team. He made a commitment to not only stay updated on the latest trends in cybersecurity but also to foster a culture of learning within his team. This included regular training sessions, workshops, and attending industry conferences. Nick also began to see the value in networking with other CISOs, recognizing that sharing experiences and strategies with his peers could provide valuable insights and new approaches to the challenges he faced.

2. Strengthening Relationships:

- Nick aimed to deepen his relationships with the board members, continuing to engage in one-on-one conversations and addressing their evolving concerns.
- He planned to implement regular feedback loops, seeking input from the board on how to improve his communication and strategies.

Understanding that trust is built over time, Nick committed to maintaining regular, open lines of communication with the board. He decided to schedule quarterly one-on-one meetings with each board member to discuss their ongoing concerns and to keep them informed of any new developments in the cybersecurity landscape. Additionally, Nick sought to create feedback loops where board members could provide input on his presentations and strategies, ensuring that he remained aligned with their expectations and concerns.

3. **Integrating Cybersecurity with Business Strategy:**

- Nick emphasized the importance of aligning cybersecurity initiatives with the company's overall business strategy, demonstrating how these efforts support growth, innovation, and customer trust.
- He aimed to position cybersecurity as a key enabler of business success, turning it from a perceived cost center into a value driver.

Reflecting on his progress, Nick realized that the true value of cybersecurity lay in its integration with the broader business strategy. He had moved beyond viewing cybersecurity as merely a protective measure and began to see it as a key enabler of business growth and innovation. By aligning cybersecurity initiatives with the company's strategic goals, such as market expansion and customer retention, Nick positioned cybersecurity as a value driver. He was determined to continue this approach, ensuring that cybersecurity was seen not just as a necessity, but as a competitive advantage.

4. **Promoting a Culture of Cybersecurity Awareness:**

- Nick recognized the importance of fostering a culture of cybersecurity awareness throughout the organization. He planned to implement regular training and awareness programs, ensuring that all employees understood their roles in protecting the company's assets.
- He aimed to create a proactive cybersecurity culture where everyone, from the board to the frontline employees, was engaged and committed to maintaining a secure environment.

Nick knew that true cybersecurity resilience required a company-wide commitment. He began planning a series of initiatives aimed at promoting a culture of cybersecurity awareness across all levels of the organization. This included regular training sessions, phishing simulations, and workshops designed to educate employees about the role they play in protecting the company's assets. Nick was also keen on involving the board in these initiatives, believing that their active participation would underscore the importance of cybersecurity and help build a more proactive and security-conscious culture.

Conclusion

Nick's journey from a technically skilled but inexperienced CISO to a confident and trusted leader was marked by continuous learning, adaptation, and a deep commitment to understanding and addressing the board's concerns. With Kathy's guidance and the support of his team, he successfully bridged the gap between technical details and business priorities, positioning MedTech Parts for a more secure and prosperous future.

As Nick reflected on his journey, he realized that his growth as a leader was as much about personal development as it was about technical expertise. The lessons he had learned—about communication, trust, and alignment with business goals—had not only made him a more effective CISO but had also deepened his understanding of what it meant to lead. He was no longer just the technical expert in the room; he was a strategic advisor, a trusted partner, and a leader who could guide the company through the complex and ever-changing landscape of cybersecurity.

As Nick looked out at the horizon, he felt a renewed sense of purpose and determination. The challenges ahead were many, but with the lessons learned and the strategies developed, he was ready to guide MedTech Parts toward a future where cybersecurity was not just a necessity but a strategic advantage.

13

Epilogue

Nick's story is a powerful testament to the challenges and triumphs of transitioning from a technical expert to a strategic leader. His journey from initial boardroom failures to becoming a trusted advisor underscores the importance of effective communication, empathy, and understanding the business context of cybersecurity.

Reflecting on the Journey

Throughout the book, we've explored essential concepts such as bridging information asymmetry, managing the affect heuristic, building trust, and understanding the audience. Nick's one-on-one meetings with board members, his diligent preparation, and his commitment to continuous improvement all illustrate the real-world application of these principles. His journey is a reminder that effective communication is not just about conveying information, but about making it relevant, engaging, and actionable for the audience.

Nick's journey also highlights the power of resilience and adaptability. There were moments when he doubted his ability to bridge the gap between his technical expertise and the board's strategic vision. However, through persistence, reflection, and seeking guidance, he transformed these challenges into opportunities for growth. His ability to pivot, learn from feedback, and continuously refine his approach exemplifies the mindset necessary for any leader facing similar challenges.

Another key aspect of Nick's journey was his evolving relationship with his team. Initially, his interactions were task-focused, driven by the need to address immediate cybersecurity concerns. However, as he grew in his role, Nick began to see the importance of fostering a collaborative and trust-based relationship with his team. He learned that effective leadership is not just about directing tasks but about empowering

DOI: 10.1201/9781003597407-13

others, encouraging open communication, and building a team culture that values shared responsibility and continuous improvement.

Acknowledging the Reality of the Journey

While Nick's transformation in this story unfolds over a relatively short period, it's important to recognize that developing these skills in the real world often takes much longer. The rapid progression in Nick's story is designed to highlight the key learning points and strategies in a compressed timeline for the sake of narrative clarity and engagement.

In reality, the journey to becoming a trusted advisor and effective communicator is rarely linear. It involves navigating setbacks, learning from mistakes, and often revisiting foundational principles as new challenges arise. For many professionals, the road is marked by periods of intense learning, followed by moments of consolidation where the focus shifts from acquiring new knowledge to refining and applying what has been learned.

It's also important to acknowledge the emotional aspect of this journey. Transitioning from a technical role to a leadership position can be daunting, filled with moments of self-doubt and uncertainty. Nick's story reflects this reality, and while his successes are highlighted, it's crucial to remember that behind every success are countless hours of hard work, reflection, and, at times, struggle. The development of communication and leadership skills is as much about emotional resilience as it is about intellectual growth.

In the cybersecurity field, the stakes are high, and the pressure to perform can be intense. Nick's story is a reminder that while rapid progress is possible, it's essential to approach this journey with patience and self-compassion. Mastery of these skills is not achieved overnight, and it's perfectly normal for professionals to take years, even decades, to fully develop the level of expertise and confidence needed to excel in boardroom settings.

Continuous Learning and Improvement

Developing these communication skills requires dedication and a willingness to adapt and evolve. It's essential to seek feedback, engage in self-reflection, and remain open to new approaches and ideas. Building trust with executive leadership and effectively communicating complex technical information in a business context are skills that grow and mature with each experience.

In addition to self-reflection, continuous learning often involves seeking out new experiences that push the boundaries of your current capabilities. For Nick, this meant stepping outside of his comfort zone, whether it was engaging in challenging conversations with board members, participating in professional development opportunities, or seeking mentorship from experienced leaders like Kathy. These experiences not only enhanced his skills but also broadened his perspective, enabling him to see cybersecurity not just as a technical discipline but as a critical component of business strategy and risk management.

The role of mentorship in Nick's journey cannot be overstated. Kathy's guidance provided him with the insights and support he needed to navigate complex situations. Mentorship, whether formal or informal, plays a crucial role in the development of any leader. It offers a safe space to explore ideas, gain new perspectives, and receive constructive feedback. As you progress in your own journey, consider both seeking mentors who can guide you and offering mentorship to others who are earlier in their career paths. This reciprocal process of learning and teaching enriches the entire professional community and helps build a culture of continuous improvement.

It's also important to recognize that the skills and strategies discussed in this book are not static. The fields of cybersecurity and business are constantly evolving, and what works today may need to be adapted or even overhauled tomorrow. Staying current with industry trends, engaging in lifelong learning, and being open to change are essential components of sustained success. Nick's story serves as a reminder that the journey of growth and improvement is ongoing, with each new challenge offering an opportunity to learn, adapt, and excel.

Final Reflections

I hope Nick's story serves as both an inspiration and a practical guide for those on a similar path. Remember that the journey to becoming a trusted advisor and effective communicator is unique for everyone, and it's okay to take the time needed to develop these skills fully.

As you reflect on Nick's journey, consider how these lessons apply to your own professional context. What challenges are you currently facing that require you to bridge the gap between technical expertise and strategic leadership? How can you apply the principles of effective communication, empathy, and audience understanding in your own work? Remember that every challenge is an opportunity to grow, and every interaction is a chance to build trust and demonstrate your value as a leader.

Nick's story also underscores the importance of balancing technical proficiency with strategic vision. As cybersecurity continues to play an increasingly critical role in business success, professionals who can navigate both the technical and strategic realms will be in high demand. This dual focus not only enhances your effectiveness as a leader but also positions you as a valuable asset to any organization.

As the author, I want to acknowledge that I am still on this journey myself. Every interaction with a board member, every presentation, and every strategic decision provides an opportunity to learn and improve. The skills and strategies presented in this book are not a one-time achievement but an ongoing pursuit.

Thank you for joining me on this exploration of cybersecurity leadership and communication. May your journey be as rewarding and enlightening as Nick's, and may you continue to grow and succeed in your professional endeavors.

As you move forward, remember that the path to becoming an effective leader is not a destination but a continuous journey. Embrace the challenges, celebrate the successes, and remain committed to your growth and development. The insights and strategies you've gained from this book are just the beginning. Continue to seek out new learning opportunities, engage with mentors, and refine your approach as you navigate the complexities of cybersecurity and business leadership. Your journey, like Nick's, is a testament to the power of perseverance, continuous learning, and the pursuit of excellence.

References

1. Amin, Z. (2019). A practical road map for assessing cyber risk. *Journal of Risk Research*, *22*(1), 32–43. https://doi.org/10.1080/13669877.2017.1351467
2. B, S., & Carr, M. (2018). *Cyber metrics: Getting the conversation straight between technical and non-technical actors*. Research Institute in Science of Cyber Security. https://discovery.ucl.ac.uk/id/eprint/10063231/
3. Bergh, D. D., Ketchen, D. J., Orlandi, I., Heugens, P. P., & Boyd, B. K. (2019). Information asymmetry in management research: Past accomplishments and future opportunities. *Journal of Management*, *45*(1), 122–158. https://doi.org/10.1177/0149206318798026
4. Blum, D. (2020). Manage risk in the language of business. In *Rational cybersecurity for business: The security leaders' guide to business alignment* (pp. 123–156). Apress. http://doi.org/10.1007/978-1-4842-5952-8_5
5. Brennan, N. M., Kirwan, C. E., & Redmond, J. (2016). Accountability processes in boardrooms. *Accounting, Auditing & Accountability Journal*, *29*(1), 135–164. https://doi.org/10.1108/aaaj-10-2013-1505
6. Buelow, M. T., Jungers, M. K., & Chadwick, K. R. (2019). Manipulating the decision making process: Influencing a "gut" reaction. *Journal of Clinical & Experimental Neuropsychology*, *41*(10), 1097–1113. https://doi.org/10.1080/13803395.2019.1662374
7. Cox, L. (2008). What's wrong with risk matrices? *Risk Analysis*, *28*(2), 497–512. https://doi.org/10.1111/j.1539-6924.2008.01030.x
8. Finucane, M. L., Alhakami, A., Slovic, P., & Johnson, S. M. (2000). The affect heuristic in judgments of risks and benefits. *Journal of Behavioral Decision Making*, *13*(1), 1–17. https://doi.org/10.1002/(sici)1099-0771(200001/03)13:1<1::aid-bdm333>3.0.co;2-s

9. Gasper, K., Spencer, L. A., & Hu, D. (2019). Does neutral affect exist? How challenging three beliefs about neutral affect can advance affective research. *Frontiers in Psychology*, 10. https://doi.org/10.3389/fpsyg.2019.02476

10. Hooper, V., & McKissack, J. (2016). The emerging role of the CISO. *Business Horizons*, 59(6), 585–591. https://doi.org/10.1016/j.bushor.2016.07.004

11. Hubbard, D. W., & Seiersen, R. (2016). *How to measure anything in cyber-security risk.* John Wiley & Sons. https://doi.org/10.1002/9781119162315

12. In re Caremark Int'l Inc. Derivative Litig., 698 A.2d 959, 971 (Del. Ch.1996)

13. Keskin, O. F., Caramancion, K. M., Tatar, I., Raza, O., & Tatar, U. (2021). Cyber third-party risk management: A comparison of non-intrusive risk scoring reports. *Electronics*, 10(10), 1168. https://doi.org/10.3390/electronics10101168

14. Kohlhoffer-Mizser, C. (2019). Conflict management-resolution based on trust? *Ekonomicko-manazerske spektrum*, 13(1), 72–82. https://doi.org/10.26552/ems.2019.1.72-82

15. Joseph, D. L., Chan, M. Y., Heintzelman, S. J., Tay, L., Diener, E., & Scotney, V. S. (2020). The manipulation of affect: A meta-analysis of affect induction procedures. *Psychological Bulletin*, 146(4), 355–375. https://doi.org/10.1037/bul0000224.supp

16. Machynska, N., & Boiko, H. (2020). Andragogy – The science of adult education: Theoretical aspects. *Journal of Innovation in Psychology, Education & Didactics*, 24(1), 25–34. https://www.proquest.com/scholarly-journals/andragogy-science-adult-education-theoretical/docview/2479494712/se-2?accountid=201395

17. Peters, E., Västfjäll, D., Gärling, T., & Slovic, P. (2006). Affect and decision making: A "hot" topic. *Journal of Behavioral Decision Making*, 19(2), 79–85. https://doi.org/10.1002/bdm.528

18. Ramu, G. (2021). To the point: ISO/FDIS 10014 incorporates the language of business to help top management understand its intent. *Quality Progress*, 54(4), 56–59. https://www.proquest.com/magazines/point/docview/2512816997/se-2

19. Roldán-Molina, G., Almache-Cueva, M., Silva-Rabadão, C., Yevseyeva, I., & Basto-Fernandes, V. (2017). A comparison of cybersecurity risk analysis tools. *Procedia Computer Science*, 121, 568–575. https://doi.org/10.1016/j.procs.2017.11.075

20. Rowe, J. (1998). No such thing as…the language of business: Colourless green ideas sleep furiously. *Management Decision*, 36(2), 117. https://doi.org/10.1108/00251749810204205

21. Shetty, S., McShane, M., Zhang, L., Kesan, J. P., Kamhoua, C. A., Kwiat, K., & Njilla, L. L. (2018). Reducing informational disadvantages to improve cyber risk management. *Geneva Papers on Risk & Insurance*, 43(2), 224–238. http://doi.org/10.1057/s41288-018-0078-3

22. Stone v. Ritter – 911 A.2d 362 (Del. 2006).

23. Van Schaik, P., Renaud, K., Wilson, C., Jansen, J., & Onibokun, J. (2020). Risk as affect: The affect heuristic in cybersecurity. *Computers & Security*, *90*, 101651. https://doi.org/10.1016/j.cose.2019.101651
24. Wachnik, B. (2014). Reducing information asymmetry in IT projects. *Informatyka Ekonomiczna*, *31*, 212–222. https://doi.org/10.15611/ie.2014.1.17
25. Wu, L., Zeng, S., & Wu, Y. (2018). Affect heuristic and format effect in risk perception. Social *Behavior and Personality: An International Journal*, *46*(8), 1331–1344. https://doi.org/10.2224/sbp.6957

Printed in the United States
by Baker & Taylor Publisher Services

Printed in the United States
by Baker & Taylor Publisher Services